IF IT RUNS IN YOUR FAMILY

HEART
DISEASE

REDUCING YOUR RISK

IF IT RUNS IN YOUR FAMILY

HEART DISEASE

REDUCING YOUR RISK

Charles Klieman, M.D., and Kevin Osborn

Developed by The Philip Lief Group, Inc.

BANTAM BOOKS
NEW YORK · TORONTO · LONDON · SYDNEY · AUCKLAND

This book is not intended as a substitute for the medical advice of physicians. The reader should regularly consult a physician in matters relating to his or her health and particularly with respect to any symptoms which may require diagnosis or medical attention. Readers should also speak with their own doctors about their own individual needs before starting any diet or fitness program. Consulting one's personal physician about diet and exercise is especially important if the reader is on any medication or is already under medical care for any illness.

IF IT RUNS IN YOUR FAMILY: HEART DISEASE
A Bantam Book / April 1991

Library of Congress Cataloging-in-Publication Data
Klieman, Charles.
   If it runs in your family : heart disease : reducing your risk /
Charles Klieman and Kevin Osborn.
   p.   cm.
Includes bibliographical references.
ISBN 0-553-34954-6
   1. Coronary heart disease—Prevention.   2. Coronary heart disease—Risk factors.   I. Osborn, Kevin, 1959–   . II. Title.
RC685.C6K58   1991
616.1'2305—dc20   90-43302
                                                           CIP

Published simultaneously in the United States and Canada

PRINTED IN THE UNITED STATES OF AMERICA

OPM   0   9   8   7   6   5   4   3   2   1

Dedicated to my parents
Paul and Harriet Klieman

—C. K.

To Marjorie Phipps Osborn, who can now worry a little less about her children's risk of developing heart disease.

—K. O.

Acknowledgments

I would like to thank the staff of the Philip Lief Group who asked me to write this book and who worked so diligently to bring it to completion. In particular I would like to acknowledge the late Jamie Rothstein who worked closely with me as the editor of this manuscript.

I would also like to thank Karen Long, an enthusiastic and bright genetics student, for her assistance.

—C. K.

I would like to acknowledge and warmly thank those who have contributed so much to this book: Doris B. Drakefield, R.N., and Irving S. Siegel, for their generous support and research assistance; Gregory Shatan, for his invaluable advice and counsel; and Susan Kiley, for her infinite patience and understanding.

—K. O.

Contents

Preface

For many years the causes of atherosclerosis, or hardening of the arteries, have been apparent. In the 1960s, researchers discovered that smoking, high cholesterol, high blood pressure, and stress all had something to do with this process. During the decade of the 1960s, famous studies such as the Framingham report pointed out the association of certain of these risk factors to heart attacks. This was reassuring information because a half million people a year die of coronary artery disease and 50 percent of them suffer heart attacks without any symptoms. Only 30 percent of these hundreds of thousands of victims have any warning; that symptom is angina (chest pain). This is why knowing the causes of atherosclerosis and preventing them is so important.

During that same period, the surgeon general of the United

States issued his first warning on smoking: It was found to cause lung cancer. Scientists soon linked cigarette smoking to heart disease, but it would be many years from that first report until the surgeon general plastered warnings to this effect on cigarette packages and in advertising.

During the 1970s, X-ray angiography was perfected and showed us the vascular damage caused by atherosclerosis. Also the techniques of bypass surgery were fully developed and there emerged a satisfactory surgical treatment for the tens of thousands of victims of this epidemic. Because of the excitement about this new technology, the press and medical community focused on diagnosis and treatment more than prevention. Hundreds of studies were gathering statistics on the causes of coronary artery disease and hundreds of other studies were being done to evaluate the results of medical versus surgical treatments. But *prevention* was just beginning to gain attention.

During this period the American Heart Association focused on one of these causative risk factors, hypertension. They were rewarded with great success. Hypertension became easy to diagnose. Medications proliferated for its treatment and millions of patients were spared the early catastrophes of stroke and heart attack.

During the 1980s a revolution was in the making; it focused on the control of risk factors to prevent heart disease. The studies begun years earlier were coming to maturity. It was conclusively proven that smoking, hypertension, cholesterol, hostility, diabetes, and genetic predisposition all contributed to the destruction of the vascular system. It was also conclusively proven by many of these studies that most of these risk factors were preventable or controllable and that with a proper lifestyle of diet and exercise we could expect to live out our normal life span without experiencing heart disease.

If we did develop the disease, new surgical treatments with lasers, atherectomy devices, and open heart surgery gave the physician a wide range of therapeutic choices. New drugs emerged to lower cholesterol and to rapidly dissolve blood clots.

During the past two decades we have become a nation of joggers, bicyclers, vitamin ingesters, vegetarians, stress reducers, and nonsmokers. Millions of us try to live the healthy life. But millions more ignore the warning signs of atherosclerosis that if heeded would enable them to prevent the onset of the disease. And millions of others are at risk of developing heart disease later in life due to family inheritance and unhealthy living habits. We've all heard that a healthy lifestyle leads to a healthier and longer life . . . but does it really?

In the last year many of our cherished beliefs have been challenged. Do we live longer if we exercise? Does it matter what our cholesterol level is? Is it better to have a Type A personality than a Type B? Is hypertension on its own really a risk factor?

Just when we thought we had a firm grasp on these issues, it seems like new information makes things more complicated than ever. But, in reality, our expanded knowledge has enabled us to define the risk factors with greater precision. For example, it may not be cholesterol per se, but low-density lipoprotein (LDL) cholesterol that is important. It may not be that all stress contributes to heart disease, but how it is handled that matters.

It is necessary to put all this information into perspective for the 1990s. *If It Runs in Your Family: Heart Disease* examines some of the controversies and presents the current thinking on prevention and treatment. The good news is that

much of atherosclerosis is preventable, and this book de-
scribes how. The answers aren't drastic or overwhelming:
simply by following a sensible diet, exercising regularly, and
controlling certain risk factors you can greatly reduce your
chances of ever having heart disease. Simply by reading this
book, you're taking a first step in that direction. Because the
typical heart attack victim is male, the pronoun *he* will be
used throughout the book; however, unless otherwise noted,
the information here pertains to women as well as men.

1

What It Means to Be at Risk

Do you know your risk of coronary heart disease? Are you at high, moderate, or low risk of suffering a heart attack? Because more people in the United States die from heart attacks than from any other cause, the answer to these questions could be extremely important to you. More than 1.5 million Americans suffer heart attacks each year, and more than 540,000 of them die of the disease. That's one death for every minute of every day of the year. Far too many of these victims are or were unaware that they had a heart problem.

If you are aware of your risk, however, you can take preventive steps to help reduce your chances of succumbing to coronary heart disease. The following quiz can help you elucidate this risk. The results can serve to guide you toward a healthier lifestyle. Although we cannot control some factors, such as family history, sex, age, and race, most of the factors that contribute to the high risk of heart disease are entirely under our control.

Quiz: Assess Your Risk of Coronary Heart Disease

Answer yes or no to the following questions.

I. *Uncontrollable Risk Factors* (examined in detail in chapter 2).
  1. Do you have a family history of heart attacks? _____
  2. Did anyone in your immediate family—siblings, parents, or grandparents—have a heart attack before age sixty-five? _____
  3. Are you male? _____
  4. Are you older than fifty-five? _____

II. *Controllable Risk Factors* (examined in detail in chapter 3).

A. Primary Risk Factors
  5. Do you smoke cigarettes? _____
  6. Is your cholesterol higher than 200? _____
  7. Is your blood pressure above 140/90? _____
B. Secondary Risk Factors
  8. Are you more than 30 pounds overweight? _____
  9. Do you exercise less than three times a week? _____
  10. Do you have diabetes, any symptoms of diabetes, or a family history of diabetes? _____
  11. Is your lifestyle stressful? _____
    and do you handle stress poorly? _____

If you have answered yes to only one of these eleven questions, you are at a relatively low risk of suffering from coronary heart disease. (Keep in mind, however, that there isn't any such thing as "no risk," particularly if you smoke.) Two to five yeses indicate moderate risk, six to nine yeses suggest high risk, and ten or eleven yeses demonstrate very high risk. Remember, just because you have a moderate or high risk of heart disease does not mean you will actually suffer from the disease. It simply indicates that you are *more likely* to develop heart trouble than people with low risk. We're not trying to scare you. Heart disease is not an inevitable part of your future. You can shift the odds more in your favor. This book will show you a number of steps you can take *now* to reduce your risk and improve your overall health.

What Is Coronary Heart Disease and Who Gets It?

Coronary heart disease, as its name implies, is a disease of the coronary arteries of the heart. It is a progressive disease that begins as early as childhood. It is the most widespread form of heart disease and occurs when the coronary arteries are blocked, a process known as atherosclerosis, or hardening of the arteries.

Atherosclerosis is a progressive buildup of cholesterol, fat, and other deposits on the inside of the arterial walls, which eventually leads to a narrowing or complete blockage of these arteries. As the coronary arteries become more and more clogged, their capacity to provide blood and oxygen to the heart muscle diminishes. It is a process that occurs in the blood vessels all over the body, but we will be focusing specifically on the blood vessels of the heart: the coronary arteries.

As atherosclerosis becomes more pronounced, symptoms may or may not occur. It is this fact that makes prevention so important. The diagnosis and treatment of coronary vascular disease can be elusive. It is possible to have severely blocked coronary arteries with absolutely no symptoms until a heart attack occurs. This condition is often called *silent ischemia* and is usually first diagnosed when a person comes into the emergency room (ER). The ER physician will ask the patient if he ever had chest pain, and the answer often will be no. That person has severe disease without symptoms. Upward of 2 million people are now suspected of having silent ischemia.

Other people suffer mild and vague symptoms such as shortness of breath and fatigue. In others, diminished oxygen supply causes chest pain—angina pectoris, a pressure in the chest due to oxygen deprivation of the heart. Still others will suffer a heart attack or sudden death, some with warning symptoms, some with none.

An estimated 6 million people in the United States currently have coronary heart disease. Although it strikes women as well as men, young people as well as old, and all races, the typical, or stereotypical, heart attack victim is a man over sixty-four years old, usually Caucasian, who has a family history of coronary disease or heart attack deaths. Family history, age, sex, and race all play a part in determining this risk. However, a large portion of this increased risk is due to behavior patterns and eating habits learned in childhood.

Age, of course, is out of our control. More than one-third of all heart attack deaths occur in people over eighty years of age, and half of all heart attacks occur in people over sixty-five. American Heart Association statistics show that the death rate from heart attacks nearly doubles each decade after the age of thirty.

As far as sex is concerned, nearly two-thirds of all heart attack deaths occur in men. The difference in risk between the sexes is thought to be due to estrogen, the principal hormone that regulates a woman's reproductive cycle. After menopause, with the decline in estrogen production, the death rate from heart disease among women begins to catch up to that of men, evening out by age sixty-five.

Race has been found to have minimal importance. Caucasian men have only a 12 percent higher risk of dying from heart attacks than do black men. But black women have an 11 percent higher heart attack death rate than Caucasian women. Asian-Americans have a lower risk than European-Americans. All in all these small differences in risk among races are not considered statistically significant. What is significant are their cultural lifestyle differences.

Most studies have shown that cultural differences in diet and lifestyle play a greater role in determining heart attack risk than do racial differences. For example, the risk among Japanese people living in the United States is greater than for Japanese people living in Japan. This difference seems to result from diet. Those individuals who maintained a traditional diet low in fats, especially saturated fats, had a very low risk regardless of where they lived. Those who adopted a more typical U.S. diet, high in saturated fats, had a higher incidence of coronary artery disease. When smoking was involved, however, the statistics evened out.

Lifestyle and diet seem largely responsible for the relatively high incidence of coronary heart disease in developed, Western countries. The first evidence of this stemmed from a five-year study of middle-aged men in seven different countries in the late 1950s and early 1960s. The Seven Countries Study, published in the *Journal of the American Medical Association,* showed that the death rate from heart attacks among men in

Finland, the United States, and the Netherlands was three to ten times greater than the rate among men in Greece, Yugoslavia, Italy, and Japan. Part of the explanation for these ethnic differences was traced to blood cholesterol levels. The men in the United States and the two Northern European countries had much higher blood cholesterol rates (averaging over 230) than those from the low-risk nations (with cholesterol rates averaging from 140 to 200). Those from the high-risk countries consumed much more saturated fat in their daily diets—from 17 to 22 percent of their total calories, compared with 3 percent in Japan and 5 to 13 percent in the Mediterranean countries.

The fact that the difference in heart disease risk among ethnicities has been traced primarily to cultural lifestyle influences rather than genetic factors is encouraging. It clearly indicates that most risk factors are under our control. So if you are already at risk, and even if you have a family history of coronary heart disease, be encouraged. Use your expanding knowledge of heart disease to make real and lasting changes in your diet and exercise habits to help ensure a long and healthy life.

Risk Factors You Can Control

The man over sixty-four years old, the one who represents the typical victim of heart attack, has a number of distinguishing characteristics. He smokes, he has high blood pressure, and he also has elevated blood cholesterol levels. It is the Framingham Study, which for more than thirty years has tracked the incidence of heart disease in 5,000 men and women living in Framingham, Massachusetts, that identified these three traits—cigarette smoking, hypertension, and high blood cholesterol levels—as the primary risk factors for heart disease.

The single biggest change you can make to reduce your risk of coronary heart disease is to quit smoking. Although there has been more attention given to smoking as a cause of lung cancer and emphysema, cigarette smoking also destroys the heart and blood vessels throughout the body. It causes arteries to clog up. The carbon monoxide and nicotine in cigarette smoking decrease the supply of oxygen that passes through the heart by way of the bloodstream. The more carbon monoxide the blood absorbs, the less oxygen it can carry. In addition, nicotine constricts blood vessels, forces the heart to work harder to circulate blood and oxygen, and raises the blood pressure and heart rate. Finally, smoking causes the blood to clot abnormally, a strong contributing factor to the clots that form at sites of atherosclerotic blockages.

High blood pressure, another of the Big Three controllable risk factors of heart disease, also makes the heart work harder to pump blood. More importantly, high blood pressure, also known as hypertension, weakens the arteries, producing tears in the inner lining of these blood vessels. The greater the pressure within the arteries, the more damage is done. Research suggests that the body responds to these tears by dispatching fat and cholesterol to "bandage" the wound. These deposits can build up and calcify, clogging the artery with atherosclerosis.

A high cholesterol level is the third major controllable heart disease risk factor. Cells throughout the body need cholesterol to manufacture hormones, cell membranes, and vitamin D. In addition, cholesterol can be transformed into bile acids, which help digest fats. To supply cholesterol to the cells that need it, small packages of fat and protein known as *lipoproteins* carry it through the bloodstream. These lipoproteins provide the basis for classifying the several forms of cholesterol that travel through the body.

The two forms that have the greatest impact on coronary heart disease are low-density lipoproteins (LDL), commonly known as "bad" cholesterol, and high-density lipoproteins (HDL), or "good" cholesterol. LDL contains a small amount of protein and a large amount of cholesterol and carries cholesterol throughout the body, depositing it where it's needed. When there is an excess of LDL cholesterol in the body, it is commonly deposited on the interior walls of the arteries, resulting in atherosclerosis.

HDL contains a large amount of protein and a small amount of cholesterol and carries cholesterol to the liver where it is excreted in the bile. *The more HDL we have the less is our risk of hardening of the arteries.* We now know that the liver produces as much cholesterol as most people need, and when we consume excess cholesterol in our diet, we create an overabundance.

Aside from the primary controllable risk factors mentioned above, there are the secondary risk factors: obesity, lack of exercise, diabetes, and stress. As will be discussed in more detail in subsequent chapters, you have an enormous amount of control over these factors and their impact on your health.

High Hopes Despite High Risk

Even if you discovered by taking the quiz at the beginning of this chapter that you are at high risk for coronary heart disease, you have plenty of reasons to be optimistic. The risk of dying from a heart attack has significantly shrunk in the last twenty-five years, and our understanding of this disease process has greatly improved. Significant advances in the prevention of coronary heart disease have saved hundreds of thousands of lives. In addition, thousands of lives have been saved due to breakthroughs in treatment. New drugs to control angina (chest pain) and decrease the work of the heart, new drugs to dissolve clots in a blocked artery during the initial phases of a heart attack, and sophisticated advances in heart surgery have all contributed to the falling mortality rate from coronary heart disease.

In deciding to read this book, you have made a commitment to expand your awareness of the risk factors for coronary heart disease. This awareness will increase your power over your own body, and will enable you to help control and prevent the ravages of this unnecessary disease process—atherosclerosis.

2

The Genetic Factors

In chapter 1, you became aware that genetic components play a part in determining your risk for coronary heart disease. This chapter investigates that risk as well as other factors not completely within your control. If heart disease runs in your family, you'll want to know all the facts in order to safeguard your family's health, as well as your own.

Research into the genetic influence on atherosclerosis has been substantial in the last decade. And most of us have actually encountered families where one member after another has died of heart attacks. Earlier work also strongly suggested the existence of this link. Nevertheless, arguments went back and forth as to whether the causes were environmental—caused by smoking and hypertension—or the result of heredity. In recent years, the causative factors have been clearly elucidated. Both genetic and environmental risk factors are responsible for atherosclerosis. One or both of these categories may exist in the life of an individual or a family. In this chapter we will focus on heredity to present a fuller picture of the causes of heart disease.

The genetic causes of atherosclerosis are being unraveled in research centers around the world. Specific areas of the chromosomes (structures in the cells that carry genes) have now been clearly associated with coronary heart disease and atherosclerosis in other blood vessels in the body, such as the carotid arteries of the neck. This work has focused on *apoproteins*, a fairly complicated subject. Basically, apoproteins are the proteins found in HDL, LDL, and other lipoproteins. They transport cholesterol to the liver and play an essential role in the metabolism of cholesterol. Their location on the chromosomes has been discovered with the use of DNA probes. (DNA contains our hereditary factors.) What this means is that specific gene sites have been identified that are responsible for the development of the numerous apoproteins. One specific apoprotein, apo B, has been associated with elevated cholesterol levels and atherosclerosis. Another cause of atherosclerosis is elevated lipoproteins, which has also shown a connection to the apo A gene.

This indicates that there are specific genetic disorders that can cause atherosclerosis. They do so by elevating cholesterol or other lipids, by promoting diabetes (a cause of heart disease), or by increasing the tendency toward obesity or hypertension.

We can hope that research eventually will lead to the development of genetic manipulations to prevent these genes from expressing themselves. An enormous amount of work is going into the Human Genome project. The goal of this study is to map out our entire genetic code. Congress has set aside $62 million for research in 1990 and $3 billion will be spent over the next fifteen years to determine the location and identity of the genes that determine our individual identities. The payoff may be tremendous. Once a gene is located, a test can be developed to determine if a particular illness will be or already has been genetically transmitted. With the research from the Human Genome project, we may be able to pinpoint those genes that can play havoc with our metabolism and cause atherosclerosis . . . and eventually we may be able to conquer the hereditary factors of atherosclerosis.

Now it is time for another evaluation to make this information on genetic inheritance applicable to your own situation.

Examining the Risk Factors You Cannot Control

Answer the following questions and score yourself accordingly.

Your Family. Did one or more of your family members have a heart attack at any age or die of a heart attack? By family members we mean a close blood relative—your parents, grandparents, siblings, aunts, and uncles.

Give yourself five points for each blood relative who had a heart attack or died of one. Add five points if both parents developed coronary heart disease before age sixty-five.

Your Sex. Give yourself five points if you are male. Give yourself five points if you are a female past menopause.

Your Age. Give yourself one point if you are under thirty years of age; three points, if you are thirty to forty; five points, if you are forty to fifty; ten points, if you are fifty to sixty;

twenty points, if you are sixty to seventy; and forty points, if you are over seventy. As you get older, your risk of developing heart disease increases whether or not there is a significant family tendency. However, if there is a family history, your risk increases even more. At the present time we can only estimate this risk, not precisely quantify it.

Scoring the Results

If you scored from one to thirty points, then the uncontrollable component of your heart disease risk is relatively low. If you scored from thirty to sixty points, you have a moderate risk of developing coronary heart disease, even before looking at the factors under your control. If you scored over sixty points, then the elements of genetics and aging alone put you at a high risk of coronary heart disease.

Obviously, these point scores can only indicate a trend. It has been well established, for instance, that if both parents develop coronary heart disease or die at an early age, the chances of the children getting the disease at an early age are increased. If only one parent develops coronary heart disease or dies at an early age the chances of the children developing the disease are not as high.

If one relative in your immediate family—a father, brother, or grandfather—had a heart attack before age sixty-five, then you have nearly a fivefold added risk of suffering a heart attack compared with someone who has no family history of heart disease. People with two immediate family members who suffer heart attacks before age fifty-five can be ten times more likely to develop coronary heart disease *at an early age* themselves than people with no family history of heart disease.

Understanding the Results of Your Self-Test

The results of this test indicate the genetic risk you might have in developing heart disease. As mentioned, other factors besides genetics contribute to our risk. Evidence indicates that part of the disparity between the sexes arises from the fact that men traditionally smoke more than women. Unfortunately, as the number of women who smoke cigarettes increases, the gender gap closes.

In contrast to sex, race itself has little or no influence on the inherited risk of coronary heart disease. Indeed—with the notable exception of Asian-Americans, referred to in chapter 1, whose lower risk of coronary heart disease may be primarily due to the preservation of traditional diets rather than to genetic factors—race seems to have little effect at all. Statistics for 1985 indicate that 185 out of every 100,000 Caucasian males who died did so as a result of a heart attack, while 165 of 100,000 black males who died suffered the same fate. Similarly, 90 of 100,000 Caucasian females who died did so as a result of coronary heart disease, while 100 of 100,000 black female deaths were a result of this disease. Whether black, white, Hispanic, Asian, or any other race, those who have a family history of coronary heart disease have a higher risk than those who don't.

But one of the biggest difficulties involved in assessing the effect of family history on heart disease risk is separating the influence of genetics from the impact of the family environment. A recent University of Utah study of 94,000 families confirmed that those individuals with a family history of coronary heart disease have five to ten times the risk of developing heart disease themselves than those with no family history of heart disease. Yet at the same time, the study found that in more than 75 percent of those high-risk families, one or more environmental high-risk factors (cigarette smoking, hypertension, or high cholesterol levels) were also present. And these additional risk factors are what stimulate or accelerate the process of atherosclerosis.

Other Genetic Factors of Coronary Heart Disease

A variety of inherited factors play a part in determining heart disease risk. Inheritance can predispose certain people to hypertension, diabetes, and high serum (blood) cholesterol, all of which increase risk. Inheritance can also determine how the body processes cholesterol. In addition, genetic factors can influence the body's ability to dissolve blood clots, common precipitators of heart attacks.

Hypertension.   Hypertension can damage the artery walls, allowing fatty deposits to build up more easily and thus lead to atherosclerosis. It also forces the heart to work harder. Statistics show that having one or both parents with hypertension increases the likelihood of developing it oneself.

Although the exact nature of the inherited predisposition to hypertension has not been determined, it is thought to have something to do with the metabolism of salt and the ability of the body to rid itself of any excess. The average American consumes three to ten times the Recommended Dietary Allowance (RDA) of salt. As a result, those people with a predisposition toward hypertension will be likely victims unless they monitor their salt intake. The National Heart, Lung and Blood Institute (NHLBI) estimates that 35 million adults in the United States suffer from hypertension and 25 million more are borderline cases. A healthy diet and lifestyle—and, if necessary, medication—can counter one's genetic predisposition to hypertension.

Diabetes Mellitus. Diabetes increases a person's chance of contracting both hypertension and atherosclerosis. At the present time approximately 5 percent of the population of the United States is diabetic and 75 percent of deaths in diabetics are due to vascular disease, primarily myocardial infarction and stroke. Two forms of diabetes occur: In Type I, or juvenile diabetes, the body does not produce the right amount of insulin. This "insulin-dependent" diabetes first shows up in childhood. In Type II, known as adult onset diabetes, the body produces the proper amount of insulin, but cells are not able to properly metabolize glucose.

The most recent research into this blood sugar disorder indicates a genetic factor that predisposes people to diabetes. (A family history for the disease can be found in 25 percent of diabetics.) Diabetes is also known to be more prevelant among certain cultures. For instance, it is nonexistent in Eskimos, but present in 40 percent of Pima Indians. This disease afflicts almost 4 million people in the United States. However, a genetic predisposition to diabetes does not always mean that you will develop it. But if a family member is being treated for diabetes, it is important that other family members have their blood sugars checked periodically to be sure they haven't developed the disease. Once diagnosed, diabetes can usually be controlled through a combination of dietary, exercise, and weight-reduction programs as well as oral medications and insulin, if needed.

High Blood Cholesterol. As discussed in chapter 1, high blood cholesterol is one of the most significant causes of heart disease. In addition, a steadily increasing body of evidence shows that a predisposition to high blood cholesterol levels (*hypercholesterolemia*) can be genetically transmitted. In particular, a disorder known as "familial hypercholesterolemia," an inability to use cholesterol efficiently, has been traced to a genetic defect. Cells throughout the body have cholesterol receptors that attract cholesterol from the bloodstream. Individuals with familial hypercholesterolemia have a decreased number of these receptors on their cell membranes. Consequently, high levels of cholesterol remain in the blood, and this excess cholesterol accelerates the development of atherosclerosis.

People who suffer from familial hypercholesterolemia have very high levels of cholesterol in their blood. If untreated with diet modification, exercise, and drug therapy these people have a significantly increased risk of heart disease, heart attacks, or sudden cardiac death before age fifty. This disorder is fortunately relatively uncommon.

Low Plasminogen Activator Levels. A recent study of heart attack victims under age forty-five at the University of Southern California found that those who had a family history of coronary artery disease also had abnormally low levels of a clot dissolver, called *plasminogen activator*. Blood clots, along with other deposits, can build up on artery walls and cause atherosclerosis. The results of this study suggest the existence of a hereditary defect that impairs the body's ability to dissolve blood clots, or conversely, an increased tendency on the part of the body to form them.

More than one of the above genetic predispositions may exist. As a result, our genetic makeup may give rise to more than one risk factor: affecting our cholesterol levels, our ability to form blood clots, and increasing our chances of developing atherosclerosis. To what extent these predispositions remain purely genetic or are significantly altered by environmental influences still remains to be demonstrated by future research.

Creating a Family Genogram: Tracing Your Family History

Creating a family genogram, an annotated family tree, can increase your awareness and provide an understanding of your family's history of disease. Even if you think you know your family history, putting it down on paper can help you establish connections among events that at first glance may seem unrelated. In constructing this family genogram, you naturally will want to focus on heart disease.

Start by drawing a family tree that spans at least four generations: yourself, your children (if you have them), your parents, and your grandparents. In preparing the "skeleton" of your family tree, you may want to use the standard genogram symbols recommended by the Task Force of the North American Primary Care Research Group and described in *Genograms in Family Assessment* by Monica McGoldrick and Randy Gerson (W. W. Norton & Co., 1985). Or you can invent any symbols you like, as long as you distinguish between male and female family members, and between those still alive and those who have died. The standard genogram symbols are

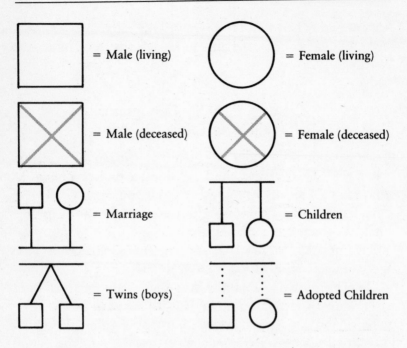

In addition to these basic symbols, you may want to draw a double line around yourself to distinguish yourself from the rest of your family. Fill in everyone's name and year of birth, as well as the year of death for those deceased. When you have finished drawing the skeleton of your family tree, you will have a diagram that resembles Figure 1.

Once you have this skeleton, you can begin adding specific notes that will help you trace your family history of coronary heart disease. Write "heart attack" next to each person who suffered a heart attack and indicate their age at the time of the incident. If the heart attack was fatal, underline the words. If known, indicate which family members suffered from angina and which were diagnosed as having atherosclerosis or

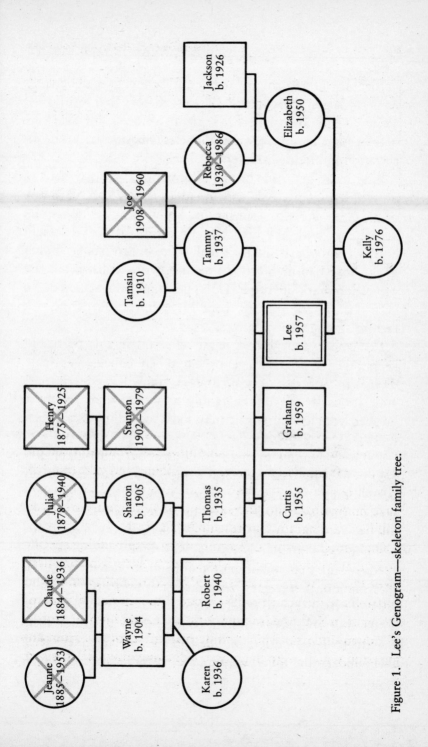

Figure 1. Lee's Genogram—skeleton family tree.

hardening of the coronary arteries. Also next to each person's name indicate any controllable risk factors that you know about. Write down whether someone smoked, for example, or had high blood pressure, diabetes, obesity, or a known elevation in blood cholesterol.

In order to get some of this information, you may need to do a little digging. Ask your relatives if they can fill in any of the holes. Perhaps your mother knows that her father and her brother both had high blood pressure, a fact you might not have known. If she isn't really sure but thinks her father might have had high blood pressure, write it down but put a question mark next to it. Don't get stuck on tracking down every last detail. Just get your best impression of the risk factors among your relatives.

Remember, only blood relations count in this particular genogram. To prepare a genogram to help educate your children as to *their* risk of heart disease, you will need to include your spouse's side of the family as well. When you have finished your genogram, it may look something like Figure 2.

Pay particular attention to the notes about controllable risk factors next to your relatives' names. See if you notice any behavioral patterns in diet or lifestyle among your immediate family. Did you "inherit" any of these habits? By concentrating on "disinheriting" these elements of your legacy, you can improve your family risk factor profile.

Make sure that you aren't the only one to benefit from this information. If coronary heart disease is present in a family, it is important that all family members have their risk profiles assessed. If you have children, educate them and teach them the rules of prevention outlined in the next chapter. Help them understand this genogram and its implications for their health.

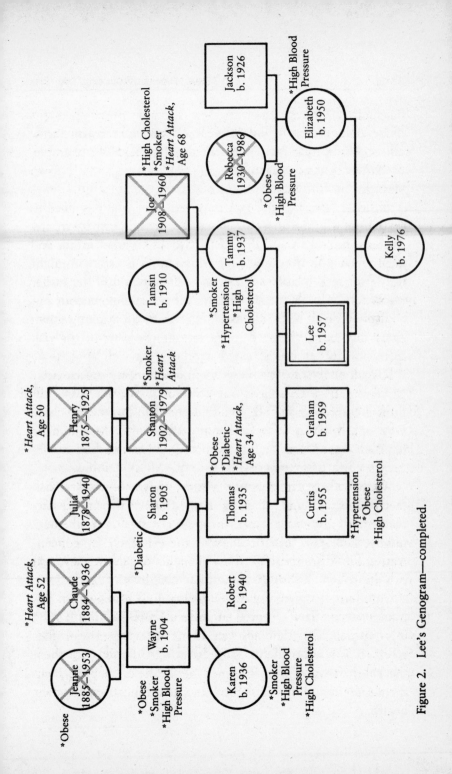

Figure 2. Lee's Genogram—completed.

Interpreting Your Genogram

The genogram can illustrate the effects of hereditary and environmental risk factors on the development of heart disease within your own family.

After you construct your family tree, certain points may be evident. For example you may find that many members of your family are obese or that they smoke or that hypertension is prevalent and that heart attacks have occurred frequently. Or you may find that your family is relatively risk free. If the risk factors are low in your family and the heart attack rate is high, then there may be a strong hereditary predisposition to heart disease. This will mean you and your family members will need to have your cholesterol, triglycerides, and other lipids tested regularly, as well as getting additional analyses of risk factors and hereditary tendencies. Actual genetic screening is not yet available, but should be in the next few years. If you find that environmental risk factors are high in your family and the heart attack rate is also high, then these factors need to be controlled or eliminated to the greatest possible extent. Many families have members with hypertension, diabetes, or who smoke. These same people are most often the ones with heart disease. Other members in the same family who live a healthier lifestyle without these risk factors for heart disease rarely have heart attacks. Look for these patterns in your own family. Armed with these facts, it should take little to convince your relatives that smoking is unhealthy, uncontrolled hypertension can be lethal, unrecognized elevated cholesterol levels can cause vascular disease, and diabetes can be devastating. These risk factors are all controllable as is the risk of the development of heart disease.

A Case History by Dr. Klieman

Alex Smith came into my office complaining of chest pain one sunny June day some years back. Alex had just moved to southern California from England. He was thirty-five. He was somewhat heavy for his five-foot, eight-inch frame and had a moderate potbelly. At first glance he appeared to be relatively healthy.

Alex related that while having sex with his wife he had been having chest pain. This had been going on for the past two months. He had seen his family doctor and an orthopedic surgeon, and they dismissed his complaints as inconsequential. An electrocardiogram (ECG), a way to evaluate the heart's activity, and chest X ray had been done and were normal. However, he continued to have chest pain and believed something was wrong.

"What makes you think it's your heart?" I asked.

"Because my father died at fifty-three of a heart attack, and my mum at forty-eight."

After careful questioning it was apparent that Alex had a strong genetic risk for heart disease. Not only had both his parents been afflicted, but so had two aunts, an uncle, and both grandmothers. His younger sister was without symptoms as far as he knew.

On physical evaluation, the only evident abnormality was a mildly elevated blood pressure. Alex underwent an extensive series of tests, including cholesterol and lipoprotein analyses, a cardiac evaluation, and an exercise treadmill test. The test results proved abnormal and a subsequent coronary angiogram (an X-ray video) showed mild coronary blockages. His total cholesterol was high, his high-density lipoproteins (HDL) were low, and his low-density lipoproteins (LDL) were high. He was thus found to have both hereditary and environmental risk factors for atherosclerosis and coronary heart disease. Fortunately Alex didn't smoke.

When he came back to my office for a follow-up visit, he was placed on a diet that significantly reduced his cholesterol intake. He also was placed on an exercise regimen that got him into normal cardiovascular condition. Follow-up visits and continued evaluations over the months showed marked improvements in his lab tests, his conditioning, and his symptoms.

Alex was scared. He didn't want to go the way of his parents. It didn't take too much counseling to alert him to the hereditary risk he had for heart disease. Alex understood that he had inherited a tendency for atherosclerosis that manifested itself with elevated cholesterol and elevated blood pressure. He was informed that with proper diet and exercise, and perhaps medication, these risk factors could be kept under control. In his case, medication wasn't required.

I recently saw Alex for the first time in six years. He is slim, nearly a vegetarian, and runs three miles a day. His cholesterol and blood pressure are normal. His exercise treadmill has reverted to normal, and, most important, he no longer has chest pain when having sex with his wife.

Alex's story shows that no one need resign themselves to being at risk for heart disease just because of family history. We may not be able to change our genetic factors, but we can do plenty to change our environmental risk. Like Alex, we can beat the odds.

3

The Environmental Factors

Now that you know the various genetic factors that play a part in determining heart disease, let's take an in-depth look at the modifiable risk factors—the ones that you can change. Again, the Big Three controllable risk factors are smoking, high blood pressure, and high cholesterol. Secondary environmental risk factors are obesity; high blood sugar level; lack of exercise; inappropriate handling of stress; as well as excessive caffeine or alcohol consumption; and the use of drugs such as cocaine, anabolic steroids, and possibly birth control pills. Both primary and secondary factors are key to modifying your risk of coronary heart disease.

As you read further, keep a pencil and a pad of paper handy. Throughout this chapter you will encounter questions designed to indicate how much certain factors influence your risk of coronary heart disease. As you come to each question, write down the question number, the subject of the question, and your score. For example: "1. Smoking, 20 points." This quick self-examination will give you further information about your general risk. Because this test takes into account only the factors you have the power to modify, it will serve to raise your consciousness about the habits and behavior patterns you should work on changing.

You may have some dangerous ways of living. Perhaps you've been smoking since your teenage years. This is the single most powerful risk factor and one that can be quickly and drastically modified. Anyone who smokes should quit completely.

1. Do You Smoke, and How Much?

The American Heart Association points to cigarette smoking as the single most important factor in death from coronary heart disease. It accounts for approximately 25 percent of all coronary deaths. Overall, smokers have almost three times the risk of dying from coronary heart disease than nonsmokers. If you are a man who smokes a pack a day, you are twice as likely as a male nonsmoker to suffer a heart attack. If you smoke two packs a day, you are five times as vulnerable. Those who smoke *more* than two packs a day can run a risk as much as ten times greater than nonsmokers who are the same sex and age. This already high risk soars even higher when combined with other risk factors.

Among women who smoke, the increased risk is even more dramatic. A recent Harvard study found that smoking as few as one to four cigarettes a day more than doubled their incidence of coronary heart disease. Those who smoked a pack a day had four times the risk of nonsmokers. And the heaviest smokers, those who smoked two or more packs a day, invited a risk a full *eleven* times higher than nonsmokers. Smoking may have a more devastating impact on women because it tends to lower estrogen levels. (Because a normal estrogen level prevents coronary heart disease, decreasing the hormone in a woman's body could increase her risk of suffering a heart attack.) In addition, women who smoke tend to have lower HDL cholesterol (the "good" kind) and higher LDL cholesterol (the "bad" kind), negating one of the most significant biochemical advantages that women have over men.

Moreover, cigarettes' carbon monoxide, which robs the lungs of oxygen, can produce an oxygen-starved heart. Angina can result, a signal of an inadequate supply of blood and oxygen.

In addition to straining and damaging the heart muscle, cigarette smoking promotes the formation of atherosclerosis. The combination of carbon monoxide and the constricting effect of nicotine injures the walls of coronary arteries. The body responds to these injuries by trying to repair them with blood platelets, LDL cholesterol, and other substances, resulting in blood clots and atherosclerotic plaques.

Scoring for Question #1. Smoking. Give yourself one point for each cigarette you smoke daily. For example, one pack a day equals twenty points.

2. How High Is Your Blood Pressure?

If you don't yet know your blood pressure, or if you had it tested more than a year ago, have it tested as soon as possible.

Everyone should have their blood pressure tested annually. If you are known to have hypertension it is probably advisable to use a home monitor to check it yourself more often—weekly, or even daily.

What does your blood pressure reading mean? The first, or higher, number (the "systolic") records the pressure in the arteries when the heart has fully contracted. The second, or lower, number (the "diastolic") measures the resistance in the vessels. The harder or thicker the vessel, the more blockage there is, and the greater the resistance to blood flow. As the heart contracts (the systolic) it pumps against blood vessels of variable thickness (the diastolic). The thicker the blood vessels become due to atherosclerosis, the harder the heart has to pump to get blood through them and the higher the blood pressure becomes—the proverbial vicious cycle.

Most physicians consider the systolic normal when it reads between 100 and 140 and the diastolic normal if it falls within the range of 60 to 90. An average blood pressure reading would be about 120/80. When an individual's blood pressure consistently reads over 140/90, that individual is considered to have hypertension. This elevated blood pressure puts additional strain on the heart and blood vessels. As many as 60 million Americans may suffer from hypertension or borderline hypertension.

Overall, people with hypertension are three to five times more vulnerable to heart disease than those with normal blood pressure. People with systolic readings greater than 150, for instance, suffer twice the incidence of heart disease as is normal. Those with a diastolic reading over 100 have a four times greater risk than people with a diastolic reading under 75. The higher the numbers, the higher the risk.

In general, the higher your blood pressure, the greater the

resistance there is to blood flow. High blood pressure thus puts extra stress on your heart. In time, this extra pressure and the force produced by the violent rush of blood propelled by the heart begins to deteriorate the inner arterial walls. The progression of atherosclerosis that results from high blood pressure may eventually lead to a heart attack. The heart, already overworked by hypertension, will have difficulty withstanding such an attack (see chapter 4 for ways to reduce blood pressure).

Scoring for Question #2. Blood Pressure.   If your systolic pressure (the first number) is above 120, take two points. Give yourself five points if your systolic pressure is between 130 and 140, eight points if it is between 141 and 160, eleven points if it is between 161 and 180, and fifteen points if it is over 180. If your diastolic pressure is higher than 80, take two points. Add five points if it is higher than 90, eight points if it is between 100 and 110, and fifteen points if it is over 110.

3. How High Is Your Total Blood Cholesterol?

Cholesterol as a risk factor has become a controversial subject. Magazines and television shows vie for attention by presenting the viewpoint either that cholesterol is a deadly risk factor or that it is harmless. *But hundreds of studies have shown the association of high cholesterol levels with atherosclerosis.* Both sides agree that cholesterol levels above 240 contribute to atherosclerosis. And most everyone agrees that cholesterol levels below 150 are ideal. The area of controversy concerns the "average" total cholesterol levels of 200 to 240: some medical researchers now feel this level is safe, while others disagree. Middle-aged men are now thought to be the significant group at risk from elevated total cholesterol.

Moreover, to clarify the issue further is the emergence of various parameters that directly affect the development of atherosclerosis *regardless of the total cholesterol level*. Recent work has identified the level of HDL cholesterol, in particular, to be a key factor. The higher the HDL, *regardless of total cholesterol level*, the lower the risk of coronary blockages or atherosclerosis showing up in other areas of the body.

The lower the pulse rate, *regardless of total cholesterol level*, the lower the incidence of coronary artery disease. Some researchers advocate taking beta-blockers routinely to keep the pulse rate low in order to minimize the effect of a higher pulse rate on the development of coronary artery disease. Obviously, it is preferable to exercise to get your cardiovascular system in shape and thereby lower your pulse rate, unless your physician advises otherwise.

Once a person passes the age of sixty, cholesterol progressively loses importance in relation to heart disease, *regardless of the total cholesterol level as long as it is not excessively high*. As you get older a little higher cholesterol is not necessarily a bad thing, but it should still be within the normal range, preferably not above 200.

The average cholesterol level in the United States and Canada is in the 220s. With each new discovery relating to cholesterol, the level acceptable to most physicians gets lower. It is thought now that if cholesterol levels can be brought below 150, atherosclerosis from cholesterol will not develop, and that if the condition has already formed, it will regress. Realistically a cholesterol count below 180 would be ideal. Below 200 is acceptable if you are thirty years old or older.

Some studies show that regardless of your age, every milligram above 200 seems to correspond to a 2 percent rise in your risk of heart disease. As cholesterol rises from 200 to 250, for example, the risk of coronary heart disease doubles (a rise of 100 percent). The risk doubles again if it continues to rise from 250 to 300.

Once you have been diagnosed with coronary artery disease, your cholesterol level is a virtual marker of your risk of future cardiac events. One study, the Multiple Risk Factor Intervention Trial (MRFIT) of 13,000 men who had coronary artery disease, which was published in the *Journal of the American Medical Association*, demonstrated that these men suffered progressive vascular disease and disability the higher their cholesterol levels, *independent* of smoking or hypertension. Obviously, smoking and hypertension made it worse, but even if the patient never smoked or had hypertension, if he had a high cholesterol level, he suffered more heart attacks.

These studies have brought us to the point where we now understand that it seems the higher our HDL cholesterol the healthier we will be and the higher our LDL cholesterol the greater our risk will be for heart disease. The final answer to the controversial issue of cholesterol and heart disease has not been decided. More research and statistical analyses are necessary before we have conclusive proof. Until then, we should continue with our commonsense approach to reducing cholesterol (see chapter 4 for details on how to lower your cholesterol).

Scoring for Question #3. Cholesterol. If your total cholesterol count is between 161 and 180 milligrams per deciliter, give yourself five points. If it is between 181 and 200, take ten points. Give yourself fifteen points if it is between 201 and 220, and twenty points if it is between 221 and 240. If your total cholesterol is over 240, take thirty points. If you don't know what your count is, I urge you to find out. A visit to the doctor for a blood test can save your life. For the purposes of this test, give yourself a fifteen if you don't know your level.

4. The Total Cholesterol-to-HDL Ratio

When your cholesterol level is taken, it is a good idea to request not only HDL and LDL levels but the total cholesterol-to-HDL ratio. A cholesterol breakdown will indicate how much of each type of cholesterol you have in your blood. It will let you know if you have an unusually high level of LDL (which would greatly increase your risk of coronary heart disease) or an unusually high level of HDL (which would actually decrease your risk).

This test, called a *lipoprotein-cholesterol fractionation,* can be taken in your physician's office or in a medical laboratory. Your doctor will advise you to fast for twelve hours before you take the test (you are allowed to drink water). A lab technician or nurse will take a small blood sample, either by pricking your finger or by using a needle to withdraw it from one of the veins in your arm. In the lab, your blood sample will be spun in a centrifuge to separate the various cholesterol and lipoproteins into different layers according to their density.

In general if your LDL levels are below 130 and you have no other contributing factors, you have a relatively low risk of contracting coronary heart disease. If your LDL count is between 130 and 160, you run a moderate risk of developing heart disease. But if your LDL count measures over 160, you are more vulnerable to heart disease. Remember, however, that cholesterol level is but one factor in heart disease. If you have low cholesterol but smoke or if your genetic risk is substantial, you are still at risk for getting heart disease.

You should take special interest in your HDL counts. Because HDL protects against coronary heart disease, the more HDL you have compared with your total cholesterol, the better. For this reason, the total cholesterol-to-HDL ratio matters. Indeed, research has shown that this ratio accurately predicts future coronary events. HDL is the important variable in this ratio. The higher your HDL, the safer you will be, even if the total cholesterol level is a bit high. If your HDL is low, then a high cholesterol level can be even more dangerous.

The National Cholesterol Education Council has established a national target of 4.5 or lower as a healthy total cholesterol-to-HDL ratio. To figure yours, take your total cholesterol count and divide it by your HDL cholesterol count. For example, if you have a total cholesterol of 210 and an HDL count of 60, your ratio would be a terrific 3.5 (210 divided by 60). If, on the other hand, you had the same HDL count, but a total cholesterol of 310, your ratio would be a risky 5.2 (310 divided by 60). If you had a 250 total cholesterol count and an HDL count of only 35, your ratio would be a very dangerous 7.1. Finally, if you had a total cholesterol of 225 and an HDL count of 50, your ratio, 4.5, would be right on target—although you could still benefit by lowering your total cholesterol.

Scoring for Question #4. Total Cholesterol-to-HDL Ratio. If your ratio is 3.5 or lower, subtract ten points. If it's over 3.5 but no higher than 4.0, subtract five points. If you calculate it to be over 4.0 but no higher than 4.5, take no points. If over 4.5 but no higher than 5.0, take five points. If over

5.0 but under 6.0, give yourself fifteen points. If 6.0 or greater, take thirty points. If you don't know your ratio, take 5 points.

5. Are You Overweight?

Obesity, defined as being 30 percent or more overweight, significantly impairs your health in a great number of ways. And although this factor isn't as significant as other risk factors, it can significantly increase your risk of developing coronary heart disease. According to findings from the Framingham Study, obese women under the age of fifty have a risk of coronary heart disease 2.5 times greater than women of average weight. Obese men face a similarly elevated risk, and this risk climbs for all people as levels of obesity increase.

Obesity may result from a combination of genetic and environmental influences including a high intake of calories and a low level of physical activity. But you can control obesity to a large extent through programs of diet and exercise. How do you know if you're overweight? Check yourself against the appropriate height and weight table, prepared by the Metropolitan Life Insurance Company (Tables 1 and 2).

Table 1. Desired Weights of Men Aged Twenty-five and Over

Height	Small Frame	Medium Frame	Large Frame
5'2"	128–134	131–141	138–150
5'3"	130–136	133–143	140–153
5'4"	132–138	135–145	142–156
5'5"	134–140	137–148	144–160
5'6"	136–142	139–151	146–164
5'7"	138–145	142–154	149–168
5'8"	140–148	145–157	152–172
5'9"	142–151	148–160	155–176
5'10"	144–154	151–163	158–180
5'11"	146–157	154–166	161–184
6'0"	149–160	157–170	164–188
6'1"	152–164	160–174	168–192
6'2"	155–168	164–178	172–197
6'3"	158–172	167–182	176–202
6'4"	162–176	171–187	181–207

Table 2. Desired Weights of Women Aged Twenty-five and Over[a]

Height	Small Frame	Medium Frame	Large Frame
4'10"	102–111	109–121	118–131
4'11"	103–113	111–123	120–134
5'0"	104–115	113–126	122–137
5'1"	106–118	115–129	125–140
5'2"	108–121	118–132	128–143
5'3"	111–124	121–135	131–147
5'4"	114–127	124–138	134–151
5'5"	117–130	127–141	137–155
5'6"	120–133	130–144	140–159
5'7"	123–136	133–147	143–163
5'8"	126–139	136–150	146–167
5'9"	129–142	139–153	149–170
5'10"	132–145	142–156	152–173
5'11"	135–148	145–159	155–176
6'0"	138–151	148–162	158–179

Courtesy Metropolitan Life Insurance Company.
[a]Women between the ages of eighteen and twenty-five should subtract 1 pound for each year under age twenty-five.

In addition, other risk factors are accentuated in the obese. One study found that overweight people from twenty to forty-four years old had 5.6 times the incidence of hypertension and 2.1 times the rate of hypercholesterolemia. Heavy people over the age of forty-five had twice the rate of hypertension as those of average weight. And this does not just apply to obese people, who are more than 30 percent overweight. If you weigh 20 percent more than your ideal body weight, you have an established health hazard. Information on proper diet and exercise follow in the next section.

Scoring for Question #5. Overweight.   Give yourself two points if you weigh more than 10 percent over your ideal weight. If you are more than 20 percent overweight, take five points. If you are more than 30 percent overweight, take nine points. Finally, if you are more than 40 percent overweight, take fifteen points.

6. Are You a Diabetic?

Diabetes mellitus has an unquestionable link to coronary heart disease. Men under age sixty with diabetes and no other risk factors have 1.4 times the incidence of coronary heart disease as nondiabetic men. Women diabetics have 2.5 times the incidence. The Framingham Study showed that men with diabetes had a risk of dying from coronary heart disease 2.3 times greater than that of nondiabetics. Again, the effects are felt even more keenly among women diabetics, who are 5.7 times more likely to die of coronary heart disease than nondiabetic women. If diabetes is combined with other risk factors, the potential impact multiplies.

Men who suffer from both diabetes and high cholesterol

levels, for example, are eight times more likely to develop coronary heart disease than diabetics who have normal cholesterol levels. And those who also smoke cigarettes push the risk up to eleven times the norm.

The presence of diabetes, or a high blood sugar level, indicates an inability of the body to process glucose (blood sugar) efficiently. Anyone with a blood sugar level higher than 120 may be characterized as a diabetic. Excessive thirst and excessive urination are two principal symptoms of diabetes. If you have these, or if diabetes runs in your family, ask your doctor to test you for it.

There are two types of diabetes: insulin dependent and noninsulin dependent. Insulin is a hormone that controls our blood sugar level. Insulin-dependent diabetes is caused by damage to the cells in the pancreas that produce insulin. This variety of diabetes, formerly called juvenile diabetes, is treated with injections of prescription insulin to compensate for the body's lack of natural insulin production. Noninsulin-dependent diabetes, sometimes called adult-onset diabetes, develops when the body becomes resistant to its own insulin. This form is usually easy to control through diet. Both types are thought to be genetically mediated.

It is important to have your blood sugar tested periodically, even if you don't think you have diabetes. If you are diagnosed as having diabetes, proper diet, exercise, and occasionally doctor-prescribed medications can help keep your diabetes under control and minimize your risk of atherosclerotic complications.

Scoring for Question #6. Diabetes. If you suffer from diabetes mellitus, add fifteen points to your total score.

7. How Much Do You Exercise?

If you have a relatively sedentary lifestyle, you're not alone. The U.S. Centers for Disease Control estimate that as many as 60 percent of all Americans are couch potatoes, engaging in little or no regular exercise. Unfortunately, as a general rule, the less physical activity you do, the greater your risk of heart disease.

The main cause of this higher risk seems to stem from a simple fact. Exercise lowers an individual's resting heart rate and strengthens the heart muscle, making it less likely that you will suffer a heart attack. And should you have a heart attack, your heart will be better able to withstand it. People who avoid exercise have a resting heart rate as much as 25 percent higher than those who exercise regularly. This accelerated heart rate forces the heart muscle to work much harder on a day-to-day basis. (The heart of a person whose pulse averages eighty beats per minute beats almost 30,000 more times per day than the heart of a person with a pulse rate of sixty beats per minute!) Those who exercise regularly also have hearts prepared to handle the strain of exertional tasks such as racing to catch a train or running up stairs.

People with sedentary lifestyles tend to have HDL cholesterol levels as much as 33 percent lower than those who exercise regularly. Couch potatoes also miss out on the other rewards of exercise: decreased blood pressure, weight loss due to burned calories, a sense of well-being, and often lower levels of blood sugar among diabetics. Finally, because exercise may actually widen coronary arteries, thereby easing the impact of any atherosclerotic narrowing that does occur, those who don't exercise probably suffer more from ischemia (lack of oxygen to the cells) than those who get enough exercise. For these reasons, many heart attacks might be prevented if only potential victims of heart disease would begin reaping the benefits of physical activity.

Exercise can be anything from walking to aerobics and from biking to basketball. Before starting any exercise program, consult your physician to make sure you have no preexisting medical conditions that might make these activities risky. (Chapter 4 provides more details.)

Scoring for Question #7. Exercise. If you exercise three or more times a week, for more than 30 minutes at a time, don't take any points. If you exercise once or twice a week, give yourself five points. If you exercise infrequently take ten points, and if you never exercise, give yourself fifteen points.

8. How Stressful Is Your Occupation?

A number of studies have established a link between the stress of your job, your personality type, the way you deal with stress, and the risk of developing coronary heart disease. The actual responsibility of the job has little bearing. It is the feeling of control you have over it that counts. Occupations that place high demands on workers but give them little control in the workplace are linked to a higher incidence of coronary heart disease. In fact, workers who hold the *least* on-the-job decision-making power have a risk of suffering a heart attack significantly higher than white-collar executives, professionals, and others who have a great deal of job control.

It has become evident in recent years that high-stress jobs that demand attention to meticulous detail are not in themselves perceived as stressful when a person is happy performing the task. For example, surgeons are noted to be happy in the operating room where they have control over their activities. It is outside the operating theater when issues in medicine seem out of their control—hospital politics, government interference in medicine, and adversarial relationships with public or private insurers—that the specialty of surgery suddenly seems stressful. Most of us experience similar feelings of stress and even hostility in response to certain aspects of our jobs, whereas other parts we find satisfying and challenging. The extent to which we cope effectively with the stressful aspects and minimize our hostility will determine in large part the contribution of stress to the development of atherosclerosis.

Another example of high stress has been found among working mothers who must make money, take care of their children at night, and, if married, play the part of a traditional wife. These women are suffering an increased incidence of heart disease. It also has been shown that the more overtime required of workers with little supervisory responsibility (another factor that usually remains out of an employee's control), the greater the incidence of heart attacks.

Unfortunately, although job stress is theoretically modifiable, you may not have the opportunity to trade your job in for something less taxing. And fewer and fewer jobs available today offer a high degree of control and a low amount of stress. Naturally, the extent to which stress alone—without other risk factors—contributes to heart attacks is still being studied. But there is little doubt that hostility in response to stress control is squeezing our coronaries. For more on what to do about stress, see chapter 4.

Scoring for Question #8. Job Stress. If you have a job that provides you with a good deal of responsibility and control, don't give yourself any points. If you have a job that involves little responsibility or control, give yourself three points.

9. How Do You Handle Stress? (Personality Types)

Stress in response to the demands placed on us by jobs, family, or life's circumstances is not always a bad thing. People react to stress in different ways according to their personality types, and these reactions may increase or diminish their risk of heart disease. Some people push back hard at stress with hostility. Others respond positively, using it to motivate them. Still others respond more casually and try not to get too worked up about the momentary vicissitudes of life.

The way our personalities respond to stress may affect our physical health. Our bodies instinctively respond to momentary anxiety, fear, and anger in ways that, *if they were to persist*, would almost definitely increase our risk of heart disease. Fortunately, however, these physiological reactions tend to cease when the momentary anxiety has passed. Adrenaline, a hormone released in large amounts during stressful or anxious moments, can raise an individual's blood pressure, especially if he already suffers from hypertension. In addition, adrenaline speeds the heart rate and prompts the liver to deposit cholesterol and fatty acids—which the body may need as fuel in this stressful emergency—into the bloodstream. Indeed, for those who've already developed heart disease, these physiological reactions to stress may bring on an angina attack by increasing the heart rate or constricting partially blocked coronary arteries.

To help determine the relative risk of heart disease for different personalities, Dr. Meyer Friedman and Dr. Ray Rosenman defined two personality types in the 1950s. They defined Type A personalities as fast-paced, impatient, aggressive, and competitive go-getters; people intensely time conscious and ambitious. In contrast, they defined Type B personalities as more relaxed, easygoing, laid-back, and seemingly unflappable. Of course, people do not tend to exhibit the behavior of their personality type *solely* in response to stress. They demonstrate it continually throughout their life. Most of us fall somewhere in between these two extremes, having a little bit of both Type A and Type B.

Initial research by Friedman and Rosenman as well as others suggested that people considered predominantly Type A had a risk of developing coronary heart disease two to three times greater than a Type B personality. However, more recent research focusing on specific traits of Type A behavior indicates that of all Type A characteristics, *only hostility* seems to be related to a high incidence of heart disease. Type A personalities who manifest their drive to succeed through hostility, aggression, and cynical distrust may have twice the risk of coronary heart disease. But other Type A personalities—confident, emotionally expressive, and always on the move—may in fact have a *lower* risk of heart disease than Type B personalities.

A Case History by Dr. Klieman

A friend of mine, a physician, is now selling ice cream in a ski resort. A few years ago he suffered a heart attack that almost killed him. In his mind and those of his physicians, his heart attack was avoidable. He had been in practice for nearly twenty years. During that time he was not only extremely driven to succeed, but manifested this drive in his

behavior. He started work at 7:00 A.M. and ended near 9:00
P.M. During those frenetic hours he saw patients in his two
offices, made rounds at three hospitals, attended the numerous meetings required of each hospital, wrote articles for
journals in his specialty, and spoke at local organizations. He
was constantly in a hurry. His car keys were in his hand as
he rushed from place to place. His patients got rushed treatment. He had little time for all the paperwork and spent extra
hours trying to keep up. The hospitals finally came after him
for inadequate chart documentation, and he had a number
of malpractice cases pending mostly from poor communi-
cation with patients and their families. Moreover, his family
life was falling apart. To sleep a few hours at night, he started
taking pills. To stay alert during the day, he started taking
pills. To calm down at dinner, he had a few martinis. He
became a classic burned-out dysfunctional professional, and
finally, nearly killed himself from stress. Why?

This was a man who had put himself under tremendous
pressure to succeed. He was good at what he did, but the
demands he allowed his profession to place on him caused
his life to reel out of control. His practice became too busy,
and he wouldn't take partners to alleviate the work. He became hostile toward anyone who questioned his authority.
He began to hate his life and awoke every day with feelings
of hostility. A natural progression of deterioration resulted,
until one day he stopped himself with a heart attack.

Interestingly, he had no other risk factors. He didn't smoke,
had normal blood pressure and cholesterol levels, and was
not diabetic; both his parents were alive in their seventies.
The only risk factor he seemed to have was tremendous stress.

He told me, when I ran into him in his ice-cream store,
that after his heart attack he had decided to change his lifestyle

altogether. He needed to get away from the demands of his practice. He felt that he might return to it in a few years, but since he had moved his family to the mountains and had started to exercise, his life was happier and simpler. He didn't plan to kill himself with stress.

This case clearly demonstrates that hostile, stressful behavior is dangerous and ultimately unhealthy. Many of us feel driven to succeed. There never seem to be enough hours in the day to do everything we want—or feel compelled—to do. We may drink too much, eat poorly, sleep too little, and never relax. Our personal lives may be strictly back-burner affairs, and we may feel lonely, angry, and hopeless. If so, we may need to make some changes. I am not telling you to quit your job and sell ice cream but to be aware of the damage stress can do to your body.

Do you fume when stuck on a slow line in the supermarket? Do you use your car horn at the slightest provocation? Do you snap at difficult business associates? Do you throw things in anger? These and many other behaviors can indicate a high level of hostility that might contribute to your risk of heart disease.

Scoring for Question #9. Personality Type.   Ask yourself whether you have a great deal of hostility or distrust. If you answer this question with a yes, take five points.

10. Drug Use, Alcohol, Caffeine, and Birth Control Pills

Certain legal and illegal drugs, but especially cocaine and anabolic steroids, directly damage the heart. A great number of studies have linked cocaine use to a higher incidence of heart attack, angina, irregular heartbeats (arrhythmias), and sudden cardiac death. Virtually every other addictive drug—derived from opium, marijuana, and cocaine—has also been implicated as having the same damaging effects. Anabolic steroids may also cause heart damage. Steroids have become increasingly popular in recent years, particularly among athletes who want to bulk up. Studies of steroid users have demonstrated that steroids significantly decrease HDL levels and elevate the total cholesterol-to-HDL ratio significantly. Naturally, this increases the chances of atherosclerosis and of suffering a heart attack.

Excessive consumption of both alcohol and caffeine may also have an impact on your risk of developing heart disease. Frequent excessive alcohol intake, more than 3 to 4 ounces at a time, tends to increase blood pressure and heart rate and may cause arrhythmias or damage the heart muscle. In addition, alcohol has a high caloric count and can, therefore, contribute to obesity. Although excessive drinking heightens your risk of heart disease, a small amount of alcohol may, curiously, lower your risk. One Harvard study, for example, found that light drinkers had a lower incidence of heart disease than abstainers. One to 2 ounces of alcohol consumed daily may actually *lower* total cholesterol and increase HDL cholesterol. This does not mean you should run out and start drinking, but if you do, do so lightly.

Studies aimed at establishing a link between caffeine consumption and heart-attack risk have shown contradictory results. We do know that large amounts of caffeine can increase an individual's blood pressure and heart rate. Depending on the individual's sensitivity, this can be as little as four cups of coffee a day. One study has shown that drinking five to six cups of coffee daily can also contribute to a high total cholesterol count. So if you drink coffee at all, try to drink it as you would alcohol, in moderation.

Evidence linking birth control pills to heart attacks also has been somewhat mixed. The pill may have an adverse effect, especially among women over forty. Although some studies have established little or no correlation between oral contraceptives and heart attack risk, others have shown that women aged thirty to thirty-nine who take the pill may have a risk as much as three times greater than those who don't. And women from age forty to forty-four who take birth control pills may have an even greater risk. The main reason is that birth control pills tend to promote blood clotting, which can be the precipitating cause of a heart attack.

Risks from taking the pill are compounded when primary risk factors—smoking, high blood pressure, and high cholesterol—are present. Women thirty years old or older who smoke and take oral contraceptives are *ten times* more vulnerable to heart attacks than women who use the pill but don't smoke. The combination seems to decrease radically the production of *prostacyclin*, a hormone produced by the lining cells of the blood vessel wall. This hormone inhibits the clumping of blood platelets and decreases blood clots. As prostacyclin decreases, blood clotting increases.

Scoring for Question #10. Drugs, Alcohol, Caffeine, and Birth Control Pills. If you use cocaine, add fifteen points to your score. If you take anabolic steroids, give yourself ten points. If you regularly drink 1 to 2 ounces of alcohol, subtract three points. If you have three or more drinks on a regular basis, take seven points. If you drink more than four cups of coffee daily, give yourself two points. If you take oral contraceptives, take four points. If you also smoke while taking oral contraceptives, take twelve points. If you are over forty years old and on the pill, take another five points.

Point Total Score Chart

Primary Risk Factors

1.	Smoking	number of cigarettes per day
2.	BP (systolic)	2, 5, 8, 11, 15
	BP (diastolic)	2, 5, 8, 11, 15
3.	Cholesterol	5, 10, 20, 30
4.	Total/HDL	$-10, -5, 5, 15, 30$

Secondary Risk Factors

5.	Overweight	2, 5, 9, 15
6.	Diabetes	15
7.	Exercise	5, 10, 15
8.	Stress	3
9.	Handling Stress	5
10.	Drugs (cocaine)	15
	Drugs (steroids)	10
	Drugs (alcohol)	$-3, 7$
	Drugs (caffeine)	2
	Drugs (the pill)	4, 5, 12

Tabulating the Results

Add up your scores from the ten questions to get your total score. Locate your total score in Table 3 to determine your level of risk for heart disease based on the controllable risk factors.

Table 3. Your Risk Based on Controllable Risk Factors

Low risk	<10 points
Moderate risk	10–30 points
High risk	30–50 points
Extreme risk	>50 points

If you scored less than ten points on this test, you are doing a very good job. Because you already have some healthy habits, you have a relatively low risk of contracting heart disease *due to controllable risk factors alone*. Keep up the good work.

If you scored ten or more points on any one question, find the cause and reduce it as a risk factor. Fortunately it's not too late to change your score. Ten points on *any* of the first four questions (including the total of both parts of question #2) means you need to pay special attention to these areas. Lowering your scores on these questions can significantly reduce your risk. Among the final eight questions, more than five points on *any* individual question also means you should be doing more to improve your odds of avoiding heart and vascular disease.

As you read chapter 4, which will help you lower your risk through prevention, focus on your own particular areas of vulnerability. After putting these preventive measures into practice for three months, take this test again to measure your improvement. You should retest yourself with these questions periodically to make sure you're staying on the right track and embracing prevention as your new way of life.

4

Lowering Your Risk *Now:* Taking Preventive Action

Now that you've evaluated your controllable risk factors, where should you begin to make changes if you've determined you're at risk? Here are the top nine choices:

- Get regular medical checkups and be aware of your blood pressure and cholesterol level.
- Quit smoking *now*.
- Alter your diet to reduce your consumption of fats, especially *saturated* fats.
- Alter your diet to reduce your consumption of cholesterol.
- If you are overweight, reduce your daily caloric intake.
- Reduce your salt intake to help reduce blood pressure.

- Add more fiber to your diet.
- Exercise regularly.
- Learn to deal with stress without hostility and distrust.

Effective prevention can be reduced to three principal behaviors:

1. Giving up smoking.
2. Eating a healthy, balanced diet.
3. Exercising on a regular basis.

By incorporating these three strategies into your life, you will reduce the impact of the three primary controllable risk factors: smoking, high blood pressure, and high cholesterol. A prudent diet and a safe, healthy program of exercise can help reduce stress, bring down your blood pressure, and lower both your total cholesterol and the ratio of total cholesterol to high-density lipoproteins (HDL). Moreover:

STUDIES HAVE SHOWN THAT PREVENTIVE MEASURES CAN NOT ONLY INHIBIT THE DEVELOPMENT OF ATHEROSCLEROSIS BUT MAY PARTIALLY REVERSE IT.

Quit Smoking

The American Heart Association regards smoking as the single most preventable cause of heart disease. Within one year of quitting, you will have significantly lowered your risk of heart disease. One study even showed that within a year after quitting HDL levels had risen to normal in some individuals.

Some evidence suggests that quitting smoking will arrest the progression of atherosclerotic plaques (lesions on the interior walls of the arteries), further decreasing your risk of coronary heart disease. Within two years, you will have cut your risk of fatal heart attack in half, even if you have already *had* a first heart attack. And within ten years you will have brought your risk back down to the level where it would have been had you never started smoking.

You can only reap these benefits, however, if you quit smoking cigarettes *entirely*. Reducing the amount you smoke or switching to a brand lower in tar and nicotine has been shown to have little or no benefit.

Smoking is more than just a nasty habit. One puff puts enough addictive nicotine into your bloodstream to provide a pleasurable stimulus to brain centers. A second puff reinforces the first, providing another stimulus and pleasurable response. Couple this with the psychological reinforcement that occurs from smoking in social situations, after meals, and under stressful circumstances and we have a physiological-psychological habit. For some people the addiction is greater than for others. Those smokers who are largely psychologically addicted have an easier time breaking the habit. They like to smoke in certain situations, but their body isn't craving the nicotine. People with a true physical addiction to nicotine have a harder time. Even when their life is at stake, when their lungs are filled with carbon monoxide, they will puff at a cigarette to their last breath. With strong determination, this habit can be broken. And that determination stems from one very simple axiom: Take responsibility for your health and your life.

Over 30 million Americans have already quit since the first surgeon general's report on smoking came out in 1964. And there are several ways to go about doing so. Keeping a "smoking journal" is one way to help increase awareness of the seriousness of your addiction. Once you decide to quit, the journal will concretely show you that the number of cigarettes smoked per day is decreasing and will encourage you to forge on until the number is zero. There are also numerous substitutions for cigarettes, such as chewing gum, mints, etc. If in spite of your best efforts you find you can't quit on your own, your local chapter of the American Heart Association or American Lung Association can suggest a stop smoking program.

The Importance of a Prudent Diet

The link between diet and heart disease has been suspected ever since World War II. The first important clue came with the elimination of food rationing in Europe after the war. During rationing, certain foods were not available, most notably meat, eggs, and butter. But when restrictions on these food types ended and a high-fat diet was more available, coronary disease became more evident. The recognition of this link helped build support and gather momentum for the Framingham Study, the Seven Countries Study, and literally thousands of other studies that have examined the connection between diet and heart disease.

These studies have amassed an indisputable body of evidence that demonstrates the connection between diet and heart disease. Today, health experts estimate that the annual death toll from heart attacks could fall from 540,000 to 440,000 if the average cholesterol level in the United States were lowered by just 10 percent. That's 100,000 lives per year that could be saved through *diet alone,* without factoring in the pluses of exercise and ceasing smoking.

Switching to a balanced, healthy diet could lower the cholesterol of most individuals with levels in the range of 200 to 240 by as much as 10 to 20 percent. Results for those with higher levels can be even more dramatic, although more restricted diets may be called for, and a doctor should be consulted. The changes you make in your diet should result in a significant lowering of your blood cholesterol *in just a few weeks.* If you have already started to have atherosclerotic buildup on your blood vessel walls, lowering your total cholesterol while raising your HDL cholesterol may help promote the regression of these fatty plaques.

Your change to a balanced, nutritious diet should accomplish five major goals:

1. Reducing your intake of fats, especially saturated fats.
2. Reducing your intake of cholesterol.
3. Reducing your intake of calories, if you have a weight problem.
4. Reducing your sodium (salt) intake.
5. Adding soluble fiber to your diet.

By accomplishing these goals, you can raise the level of HDL cholesterol in your blood, while decreasing both your total blood cholesterol count and your blood pressure.

Reducing the Intake of Fats

For the average American, fat occupies almost 40 percent of their daily intake of calories. And almost two-thirds of these calories (25 percent) come from saturated fat (see definition on pages 59–60). Since the American Heart Association recommends limiting saturated fats to 10 percent (not 25 percent) of all calories consumed, most of us are filling ourselves with more than 2.5 times as much saturated fat as we should! And, as we've said before, the amount of saturated fat a person consumes has a causal link to the level of blood cholesterol.

Most saturated fats are found in animal products, especially meat and dairy products. Red meats have a particularly high content of saturated fat, which tends to be layered throughout the meat and makes it difficult to trim. Meats, including beef, veal, pork, and lamb as well as cold cuts, hot dogs, sausages, and bacon also have a high concentration of saturated fats. Organ meats such as liver, kidneys, and brains are especially high in saturated fats. Poultry has a high saturated fat content too, but unlike fatty meats, chicken allows you to get around its fat content simply by removing the skin. Whole milk and dairy products such as ice cream, cheese, and butter, also have a high percentage of saturated fats.

Despite a common misconception, saturated fats are not limited merely to animal and dairy products. You can also find highly saturated vegetable oils. In particular, five vegetable oils have a high saturated fat content: cocoa butter, coconut oil, palm oil, palm kernel oil, and completely hydrogenated vegetable oil. Coconut and palm oils have a concentration of saturated fats ranging from 50 to 80 percent. Although few people cook with these saturated vegetable oils or consume them on their own, these fats nonetheless sneak into our diets. If you start looking for them, you will find them listed on many food packages, often as prominent ingredients in commercially baked goods such as crackers, packaged snacks, nondairy creamers, popcorn, and other processed foods. The top seven sources of saturated fats in the American diet are, in order from highest to lowest levels:

1. Hamburgers, cheeseburgers, and other ground beef dishes.
2. Whole milk, chocolate milk, and milk shakes.
3. Hard cheeses.
4. Beef steaks and beef roasts.
5. Hot dogs, ham, and cold cuts.
6. Commercially baked goods such as cookies, cakes, croissants, doughnuts, and muffins.
7. Eggs (egg yolks are the richest source of dietary cholesterol, contributing more than 35 percent of cholesterol in the American diet).

All told, these seven foods account for half of all the saturated fats eaten in the United States. So if your favorite lunch consists of a cheeseburger with bacon, french fries, a chocolate milk shake, and a handful of cookies, join the club . . . the heart attack risk club. You need to work at cutting down on these foods and even cutting some of them out of your diet entirely.

What Is Fat and What Is the Difference Between Saturated, Polyunsaturated, and Monounsaturated Fats? Fats are made up of triglycerides, which are three fatty acid chains; they are present in the body as a source and storehouse of energy. Every living thing manufactures fatty acids and assembles them in some form to store energy. Animals form *saturated* fats while plants assemble *polyunsaturated* and the less complex *monounsaturated* fats.

The terms *saturated* and *unsaturated* refer to the number of hydrogen atoms that make up the fatty acids used to manufacture these different types of fat. Saturated fatty acids contain the most number of hydrogen atoms, monounsaturated fat has less, and polyunsaturated, the fewest. The more saturated it is, the more solid the fat is at room temperature. For example, butter and lard are solid at room temperature. The less-saturated polyunsaturated and monounsaturated fats are liquid at room temperature. For instance, the softer margarines contain a larger percentage of polyunsaturated fats. The softer a margarine is, the more polyunsaturated fat it contains. Polyunsaturated fats, which are usually liquid at room temperature, are found in the seeds of plants. The oils from cottonseed, corn, safflower, sunflower, and sesame seeds are well known examples. Monounsaturated fats are found in olive oil and canola (rapeseed) oil. Almonds also have a high monounsaturated fat content.

Again, some vegetable products contain saturated fats. In addition to the oils I mentioned, when vegetable oils normally lacking saturated fats are chemically modified to make them more useful in baking, a process called hydrogenation is used, which adds hydrogen atoms to the oil. This changes some of the polyunsaturated fatty acids into saturated ones, which gives them a greater shelf life. These oils are listed as hydrogenated or partially hydrogenated vegetable oils; they are more saturated than the oils from which they were derived. Vegetable shortening and margarine are examples of partially hydrogenated or hydrogenated vegetable oils. Cooking with nonhydrogenated oils will help reduce the level of saturated fat in your diet.

Some meats contain polyunsaturated fats; fish and chicken have some polyunsaturated fats, a greater amount than red meat. Fish is especially rich in polyunsaturated fats, hence fish oil is liquid at room temperature.

This basic explanation of fat and its origins can help you intelligently pick the foods you eat. Certainly we need fat in our diet . . . just less of it than we are accustomed to consuming. And we need more of the healthier polyunsaturated and monounsaturated fats and less saturated ones.

Cholesterol and Its Relationship to Fat

We can lower our blood cholesterol if we replace the saturated fats in our diet with polyunsaturated fats. But if we simply increase polyunsaturated fats and don't decrease the saturated fats in our diet, we are just consuming more calories as fat.

A rule of thumb is that saturated fats raise our blood cholesterol. Because they suppress production of low-density lipoprotein (LDL) receptors, more LDL is left in the bloodstream, resulting in a higher level of total cholesterol.

BECAUSE POLYUNSATURATED FATS LOWER LDL AS WELL AS HDL LEVELS, WE WANT TO CONSUME THEM IN MODERATION. MONOUNSATURATED FATS, IN CONTRAST, JUST LOWER LDL AND NOT HDL.

Peanut oil, olive oil, and canola oil are excellent sources of monounsaturated fat and should be your cooking oils of choice.

The liver produces about 1,000 milligrams of cholesterol daily, which is almost all the body needs. However, the average American eats more than 500 milligrams of dietary cholesterol every day. This is twice as much as the 250 milligrams recommended by the American Heart Association.

What Foods Contain the Most Cholesterol?   One egg yolk averages about 275 milligrams of cholesterol, close to the maximum daily allowance advocated by the American Heart Association. Among poultry and red meats, those high in cholesterol include

- Chicken livers (746 milligrams per 3-ounce serving).
- Sweetbreads (396 milligrams per 3-ounce serving).
- Beef liver (372 milligrams per 3-ounce serving).
- Brains (over 2,000 milligrams per 3-ounce serving).

Among seafood, shellfish have high cholesterol levels. But they have a high polyunsaturated fat content and are, therefore, relatively safe to eat.

- Shrimp (96 milligrams per half cup).
- Lobster (90 milligrams per half cup).

It is clear from this information that the less meat we consume from whatever source, the less fat and cholesterol we will consume and the less will be our risk of heart and vascular disease. The more vegetables we eat to replace the meats, the healthier our bodies will be.

Vegetables, fruits, grains, and cereals contain no cholesterol. Nuts, although they have a high fat content, contain no cholesterol. This is why if one is a strict, nonlactovegetarian (that means not eating cheeses or milk products), nary a drop of cholesterol will cross your lips although, of course, such diets need careful monitoring. Chapter 9 includes a list of heart-healthy cookbooks for further reading about cooking with less fat and cholesterol.

Reducing Calories

The third important dietary step you can take to reduce your heart attack risk involves cutting down on the total amount of calories you consume, if you are overweight. Shedding those extra pounds could bring down your blood pressure, lower your total cholesterol count, and reduce your risk of coronary heart disease. As a bonus, weight loss will cut your risk of developing diabetes, another risk factor for coronary heart disease. Finally, weight loss has been associated with lower LDL counts and higher HDL counts, further reducing your chances of suffering from heart disease.

The most successful diets bring about a slow, steady weight loss rather than rapid losses with a crash diet or the latest fad diet. Because your body needs essential nutrients on a daily basis to operate properly, fasts, fads, crash diets, and unbalanced diets can be extremely dangerous. And although you may manage to take off some pounds with these diets, chances are you won't keep those pounds off when you go off the diet. Permanent long-term results are desired, not short-term trimmings.

It has been generally accepted in the scientific community that changing one's diet patterns resets the appetite center in the brain, called the apostat. Quick-fix diets promote resetting of the apostat to unrealistic levels too quickly. As a result, people are not able to tolerate these starvation levels for very long, and they quickly return to their previous level of calorie consumption. They may get instant gratification for a few weeks or even a few months, but the pounds quickly come back. The body is not functioning at a realistic level of food consumption, and it cannot sustain it on a long-term basis.

Moreover, starvation levels are unsafe. When your own body fat is used as a source of energy on an accelerated basis during these periods of starvation, fats quickly pour into the bloodstream and can accelerate atherosclerosis. More fat is floating around than the body can dispense with, and as we have pointed out in previous sections, such high levels of fat and cholesterol can be a dangerous risk factor for atherosclerosis. If you crash diet, you may not be taking the fat in through your mouth, but you are forcing your body to pour it into your bloodstream.

So what is the intelligent method of weight loss? Simply a diet that is consistent, gradual, and thoughtful. The best and healthiest diets are the low-fat, high-fiber diets. They minimize diet as a risk factor for the development of atherosclerosis and other diseases.

If you undergo a program of gradual calorie reduction to meet your ideal weight, in effect you are resetting the apostat in a permanent way. First you need to estimate the excess pounds you need to shed. Each pound is equivalent to 3,500 calories. If you cut down your caloric intake by 500 calories a day, you will achieve a 3,500-calorie reduction per week or 1 pound per week. In six months you will have gradually and intelligently lost 25 pounds, and you will be resetting your apostat to an acceptable long-term level. Again, refer to chapter 9 for further reading on dieting for a healthy heart.

Exercising, along with calorie reduction, naturally accelerates the weight loss process while providing additional healthful effects. And, of course, neither calorie reduction nor exercise alone is as productive as the two combined. If you have a completely sedentary life you will burn approximately 2,200 calories per day, or nearly 100 calories an hour. Without exercise you would need to limit yourself to 1,700 calories a day to lose 1 pound per week. With exercise your diet may not need to be as stringent. Depending on your exercise program, you may be able to consume 2,000 or more calories a day and still lose weight. Exercise also curbs your appetite, and once you follow the rules of an exercise program, you will get exactly what you want . . . a trim, lean, physically healthy and active body.

Moderate exercise—walking, leisurely bicycling, bowling, or square dancing—can use up 200 to 350 calories per hour. That's 100 to 250 more calories than you burn up just sitting around. And the more vigorous activities—tennis, skiing, speed cycling, and running—can burn up 400 to 900 calories an hour.

In chapter 3, we explained other benefits of exercise to the heart and to the lowering of blood pressure, cholesterol, and blood sugar levels. And we will go into more detail later in this chapter.

Important Note!

In any event, but especially if you are obese (more than 30 percent above your normal weight range), it is important to consult your physician before beginning any diet or exercise program. He or she will help you develop a plan that is appropriate for your needs and physical condition.

What Foods Contain the Most Calories?   Rich desserts—

cakes, cookies, pastries, and ice cream—have more calories than almost any other foods, usually ranging from 300 to 500 calories per serving. Among meats, poultry contains fewer calories than either fish or red meat. Red meats have the most calories of the three due to their higher fat content. Among beverages, only milk shakes (about 500 calories) and other whole milk drinks (160 to 185 calories) contain more calories than alcoholic drinks, including beer and wine, which average over 100 calories per drink. Finally, almost all fruits, vegetables, and grains contain less than 100 calories per serving, with many containing less than half that amount. Any number of books available in your supermarket and bookstore contain detailed information on the calorie content of various foods.

What's the Best Way to Cut Down on the Number of Calories Consumed? Motivation and planning will help you achieve your target weight loss goal. Reducing fats not only reduces atherosclerotic risk, but it is the best way to reduce calories. To keep calorie intake low, you will need to cut down on *all* fats whether saturated, polyunsaturated, or monounsaturated: each contain about 9 calories per gram. In contrast, carbohydrates and protein average only about 4 calories per gram. So by cutting down on fats and cholesterol, and substituting more carbohydrates (such as fruit and vegetables) and low-fat proteins (such as fish or chicken) you will be cutting down on calories.

Reducing Blood Pressure: Cutting Down on Salt
The average American consumes two to three times as much sodium as the American Heart Association recommends, and perhaps ten to twenty times as much as he or she

needs. Many people rid themselves of some of this excess sodium through perspiration and urination. For smokers, obese people, and others susceptible to hypertension, however, excess sodium can cause retention of fluids and raise blood pressure. Therefore, limiting salt intake, especially when combined with weight loss and increased exercise, can help control hypertension.

What Foods Have the Most Sodium? Did you ever eat what you thought was a low-salt meal and find yourself drinking water the rest of the night? This situation is not at all uncommon. Salad dressings, spreads, gravies, and even boiled vegetables are often prepared with too much salt. Once you start leaving salt off your food—that means never picking up the saltshaker and leaving it out of your cooking—you will find that the taste of salt can be unpleasant, actually spoiling the natural taste of the food.

Most packaged foods have a substantial salt content. Potato chips, pretzels, salted peanuts, pickles, and cured bacon have a blatant salty taste. But other foods, because they don't taste so salty, sneak their high sodium content into our diet. Processed foods, which add salt as both a preservative and a flavoring, provide the highest source of sodium in the American diet. Frozen foods and canned soups and vegetables have an especially high concentration of sodium. Dry foods, such as packaged breakfast cereals and soup mixes, also contain a great deal of sodium. Finally, process cheese and lunch meats have a high sodium content.

What's the Best Way to Cut Down on Sodium? The most effective means of lowering the amount of sodium you eat is to reduce drastically the amount of processed foods and packaged snack foods in your diet. Cook more fresh foods and fewer prepackaged or frozen foods. If you gradually lower the amount of salt you use in cooking, you will discover that just as salt is an acquired taste, so is lack of salt. Try substituting other seasonings for salt. Use more pepper, garlic (not garlic salt), onions (not onion salt), dill, and other herbs. In this way you will be able to wean yourself off salt and enjoy a healthy and tasteful alternative.

What Fiber and Starch Can Do for Your Heart

As you cut down on meats, eggs, cheese, and dairy products, substitute foods high in complex carbohydrates and fiber. We derive all of the complex carbohydrates in our diets from plants and plant products. *Whole* grains such as rice, oats, wheat, barley, and rye provide an excellent source of complex carbohydrates, as do products made from these grains: whole grain pastas, whole grain breads, and whole grain cereals. Certain fruits and vegetables, especially peas and beans, can also add complex carbohydrates to your diet. Furthermore, complex carbohydrates are quite low in calories.

A great number of studies have shown that dietary fiber, the indigestible parts of fruits, vegetables, and grains can benefit your health in several ways. There are two types of fiber. The first type is *insoluble fiber*, which, as the name implies, does not dissolve in water. It is found in whole wheat, corn, wheat and corn bran, other whole grains, and certain vegetables and fruits. This fiber, which cannot be readily absorbed in the gastrointestinal tract, provides bulk and helps both food and water travel through the intestines. Studies have shown that a diet high in insoluble fiber might also help prevent certain types of cancer, especially colon cancer.

The second type of fiber is *soluble fiber,* which is digestible and can be dissolved within your gut. Soluble fiber has been found to lower blood cholesterol levels. And this lowering of cholesterol could decrease your risk of coronary heart disease.

What Foods Contain Large Amounts of Soluble Fiber? Oats and oat bran have a great deal of soluble fiber, and have received substantial attention in recent years for their health benefits.

In addition, fresh or dried peas and beans—including kidney beans, navy beans, lima beans, split peas, garbanzo beans (chick-peas), soybeans, and lentils—all contain *guar gum,* which is a form of soluble fiber that has been shown to lower cholesterol. In fact, recent studies have shown that guar gum is more effective than oats in reducing cholesterol. Adding it to your diet every day can reduce your cholesterol levels from 10 to 20 percent.

Pectin, another form of soluble fiber, is found in most fruits, including apples, plums, nectarines, peaches, oranges, grapefruits, bananas, figs, and grapes. It has also demonstrated effectiveness in lowering blood cholesterol. Guar gum and pectin are often listed as thickeners on the labels of packaged foods.

Vegetables such as carrots, cabbage, broccoli, onions, and potatoes also contain soluble fiber.

How Does Soluble Fiber Work? A diet high in soluble fiber can lower total blood cholesterol levels by as much as 20 percent, and LDL levels by even more. How this process works is still not fully known, but researchers suggest that soluble fiber helps remove cholesterol from the body, probably by attaching itself to cholesterol-containing bile acids in the gastrointestinal tract (your stomach and intestines) and then speeding their elimination from the body. Whatever the cause, the results are clear: A significant reduction in blood cholesterol. As a bonus, like most complex carbohydrates, high-fiber foods create a feeling of fullness, which can help you cut down on your caloric intake.

How Much Fiber Is Needed to Lower Cholesterol? The average American consumes about 20 grams of fiber a day. If you double your consumption of fiber to 40 or 50 grams a day, you may lower your cholesterol level significantly. It is best to increase your fiber intake gradually, giving your gastrointestinal tract time to adjust. Start with breakfast and substitute unsweetened, whole grain cereal for eggs, and whole wheat toast for doughnuts. At snacktime, raisins, raw carrot sticks, and unsalted unbuttered popcorn (occasionally) are good substitutes for candy. Hamburgers or other lunch meats can be replaced by salads . . . and so on throughout the day.

Once you get used to eating low-fat meals that are high in fiber, the taste of fat will soon become unpalatable. Furthermore, you will feel more alert after you eat. That heavy, sleepy feeling after a fatty meal will soon be a distant memory.

Fish Oil and Your Heart

Fish, long rumored to be "brain food," may actually turn out to be heart food instead. Eskimo and Japanese populations consume enormous quantities of fish, and studies have shown that both populations have an extremely low incidence of heart disease. The type of polyunsaturated fat contained in most fish, known as omega-3 fatty acids, seems to offer protection against coronary heart disease. One study, for example, showed that a salmon-rich diet could lower blood cholesterol by as much as 15 percent, even though the subjects consumed average amounts of cholesterol (500 milligrams a day). In addition to lowering cholesterol, omega-3 may also lower blood pressure and make blood platelets—the blood's clotting component—less sticky, inhibiting their tendency to form life-threatening clots.

Which Fish Contain the Most Omega-3 Fatty Acids? Most cold-water fish have larger concentrations of omega-3 fatty acids. In general, the fattier the fish, the more omega-3 it contains. Salmon, mackerel, albacore tuna, and herring all have high concentrations. Curiously, the most popular fish in the American diet—less "fishy" fish such as flounder, cod, haddock, whiting, and other white fish—contain the least amount of omega-3 fatty acids. In addition to fish, linseed oil, canola oil, walnut oil, and soybeans also contain high concentrations of omega-3 fatty acids.

What's the Best Way to Increase Consumption of Omega-3 Fatty Acids? Eat fish! Eating tuna or salmon two or three times a week certainly wouldn't hurt your diet or the health of your heart. In addition to the possible benefits you may gain through omega-3, *all* fish is low in saturated fat. Even shellfish (especially shrimp, crab, and lobster), which has a moderately high cholesterol content, has little saturated fat, making it safe to eat on an occasional basis. However, you should probably avoid taking fish oil supplements. The proper dosage of omega-3 is not yet known, nor is the capsule content reliable. In addition, some fish oil capsules on the market actually contain cholesterol and saturated fats, negating any beneficial impact they might have.

Putting It All Together: Building a Healthy Diet

As you set out to establish healthier eating habits, first evaluate your current diet. Keep a record of everything you eat over the course of a week and use a calorie-counting guide to calculate your normal caloric intake. Then follow the American Heart Association's eating guidelines (and your physician's advice, of course) to work toward a healthier heart:

- Reduce your total fat consumption to less than 30 percent of your daily caloric intake. This should be done as follows:
    Reduce your consumption of saturated fats to less than 10 percent of your total daily calories.
    Limit polyunsaturated fats to 10 percent of your total calories.
    Use monounsaturated fats, which can comprise 10 percent of your total calories.
- Limit your consumption of dietary cholesterol to 100 milligrams per 1,000 calories, with a maximum of 250 to 300 milligrams per day. Heart-healthy cookbooks and diet books contain information that will allow you to calculate your cholesterol intake.
- Limit your sodium intake to 1 gram per 1,000 calories, not to exceed 3 grams per day.
- Limit your protein consumption to 10 to 15 percent of your total daily calories.
- Obtain 50 to 60 percent of your calories from complex carbohydrates.
- Eat plenty of fruits and vegetables.
- Increase your consumption of soluble fiber (oats and beans).

These recommendations were directed to the general public, and not specifically to those at risk of coronary heart disease. If your blood cholesterol is very high or if these suggested restrictions don't bring it down to a safe level, you may need to observe further limitations on the amount of fat and cholesterol you consume. Similarly, you may need to restrict your diet further if you have hypertension and these restrictions do not bring your blood pressure down to a safe level. Ask your doctor what else you can do.

What's the Best Way to Choose Heart-Healthy Foods? Achieving these recommended standards begins with smart shopping. Read the labels of the foods you buy. Check all ingredients. Try to avoid buying products that contain any of the five highly saturated vegetable oils: cocoa butter, coconut oil, palm oil, palm kernel oil, and completely hydrogenated vegetable oil. In addition, watch out for unspecified "vegetable oils"; this phrase usually indicates oils high in saturated fats. Check the nutritional information on the label, too. Figure out the percentage of fat in that food by multiplying the number of grams of fat listed on the label by nine and comparing that figure (the calories of fat) with the total calories.

Beware of misleading labels and advertising. Some products advertised as having no cholesterol or low cholesterol, for instance, have very high fat contents. Similarly, some cereals promoted as high-fiber also contain highly saturated coconut or palm oils. Commercially prepared granola has a higher fat content than almost any other cereal. Most low-fat milk still has a 2 percent fat content—which is certainly better than whole milk, but still twice that of 1 percent milk.

So What Are the Basic Guidelines for Eating Right? If you keep in mind a few rules of thumb, you will be well informed about the health value of your food. Dividing all food groups into two groups, vegetarian or animal, will enable you to control the amounts of fat, carbohydrate, and protein that you eat.

Vegetarian diets—not lactovegetarian (diets that include dairy products) but purely vegetarian—include all the vegetables and fruits. I believe a well-balanced vegetarian diet will give you all the sustenance a normal body needs, including vitamins and minerals. Remember that cholesterol does not exist in the world of vegetables, so if you are trying to avoid it, the vegetable kingdom is the place to be. (Again, be sure to educate yourself before starting such a diet.)

Adding cheese to the vegetarian diet adds substantial amounts of fat. Eat less cheese, but when you do, choose low-fat cheeses, especially low-fat cottage cheese, part-skim ricotta cheese, part-skim mozzarella, and Parmesan cheese. Cutting down on dairy products in general is beneficial. Using low-fat or skim milk, limiting your egg consumption to no more than two per week, and keeping your ice cream consumption under control will minimize your exposure to fat globules.

Add fiber generously to your diet. This includes beans, chestnuts, chick-peas, grains, pasta (without eggs), vegetables, and fruits (except coconut). Almonds are an excellent source of monounsaturated fats and are very helpful in reducing cholesterol. Watch out, however, for the fat- and salt-laden roasted varieties.

For those who eat meat, fish is the safest source because of its omega-3 content. Eat fish two or three times a week to get the maximum benefit from omega-3 fatty acids. Poultry is the next safest, but remove its skin and remember that white meat has less fat than dark meat. Red meat is the biggest culprit in terms of fat content. The less you eat the better.

In preparing meat, trim off the fat. With poultry you should remove the skin. Broil, bake, stew, or roast meat instead of frying it. Frying just adds more fat from the cooking oil.

And even though the cooking oil may be polyunsaturated fat, it is still fat and the less eaten the healthier your heart will be.

As you make changes in your diet, observe the rules of common sense and moderation. Savor a wide variety of foods in moderate amounts. As long as you keep your diet low in cholesterol, saturated fats, and calories, dietary risk for atherosclerosis will be minimized.

Your children would also do well to learn moderation in their diet, and you can be their shining example. Even though data to support dietary recommendations for children are controversial, their future habits need to be sculpted at an early age. Children grow rapidly and need larger amounts of food and calories than adults. How much of those calories should be from fat is unclear. Ask your pediatrician for his or her opinion.

Also, encourage your child to be active. And remember: Children pick up *your* eating habits. Even though they may ignore good eating habits while they are growing, once they become adults, they will likely remember your example. Children who grow up in families that model healthy lifestyles will have a head start on risk-prevention lifestyle for atherosclerosis.

Developing a Prudent Exercise Program

In combination with a healthy, balanced diet, a program of regular exercise will help prevent heart disease as well as improving your overall conditioning. Studies have shown a strong correlation between exercise and a lower incidence of coronary heart disease.

A moderate exercise program can in many cases keep blood pressure—both the systolic and diastolic pressures—in the normal range for people who are moderately hypertensive, thus minimizing the effect of this risk factor. People with severe cases of hypertension may be advised by their physicians to avoid strenuous activity until their blood pressure is brought under control. In addition, exercise can lower your total cholesterol level and raise your HDL levels, minimizing these risk factors.

Other benefits include burning calories and reducing weight. People who exercise regularly have less inclination to overeat or to smoke. Another fringe benefit of exercising regularly is the endorphin kick. Endorphins are produced in the brain during the period of exercise and provide a lasting feeling of health and well-being throughout the day. Once you have exercised to the level of cardiovascular conditioning and then stop exercising regularly, you will notice the sluggishness that comes from the lack of elevated endorphins. It is a noticeable difference.

Is Strenuous Exercise Needed?   Recent studies from the Institute of Aerobics Research in Dallas showed that vigorous exercise is not needed to substantially reduce your risk of heart disease. Their study of 13,000 men and women showed that simply walking at a fast pace 30 to 60 minutes daily could halve your risk of heart disease. This is one of the first studies to show that only modest exercise is needed to gain substantial benefits.

Increasing exercise to competitive athletic status does little to further reduce the risk of death from coronary artery disease. If you want to improve the condition of your heart and coronary arteries, you do not need to undergo a strenuous or physically punishing program of exercise.

IT HAS BEEN SHOWN THAT EXERCISING 30 MIN-
UTES A DAY THREE OR FOUR TIMES A WEEK WILL
GET YOU IN CARDIOVASCULAR SHAPE OVER A PE-
RIOD OF WEEKS.

That is not to say that more rigorous exercise is bad for your
heart, but only that the incidence of heart disease among those
who exercise moderately and those who exercise intensely is
not substantially different.

The most significant statistical difference in the incidence
of heart disease occurs between those who *never* exercise and
those who exercise moderately. One seven-year study at the
University of Minnesota found that the death rate among
middle-aged men *already at risk* for coronary heart disease
was 38 percent lower among those who engaged in moderate
exercise such as bicycling, dancing, and swimming (see more
examples below). A similar Harvard study observed 30 percent fewer heart attack deaths among moderately active people than among those who remained sedentary.

What's the Best Type of Exercise for the Heart?   Again,
research has shown that moderate aerobic exercise is probably the best type of exercise for the heart, although light
exercise like walking does produce definite health benefits.
Moderate exercise includes most aerobic activities such as
fast walking, jogging, running, swimming, cycling, cross-
country skiing, rowing, aerobic dancing, jumping rope, and
racquetball. Other aerobic exercises can be done at home or
in the gym using treadmills, stairmasters, stationary bicycles,
cross-country ski machines, or rowing machines.

Note: Lifting weights, although it can strengthen and tone
skeletal muscles, does not improve your aerobic fitness or
benefit your heart in any way.

To create the greatest health benefits, unless your doctor advises otherwise, aerobic exercise should aim at a target of 60 to 80 percent of the maximum heart rate. This range is very easy to calculate: first subtract your age from 220; then, to find the range you need to target through aerobic exercise, multiply your maximum heart rate by 0.6 and then by 0.8. For example, if you are forty-five years old, your maximum heart rate is 175 (220 minus 45). The optimal range for your heartbeat during exercise is therefore 105 (175 times 0.6) to 140 (175 times 0.8).

The benefits of aerobic exercise are largely those of cardiovascular conditioning. It makes your heart pump stronger and slower. By slowing your pulse by only ten beats per minute, you can save your heart almost 15,000 beats a day. This lighter workload may have important consequences: one study showed coronary deaths to be two to three times less frequent if the heart rate was 60 beats per minute rather than 80 beats per minute.

How Much Exercise Is Needed?   Consistency more than intensity is the key to gaining health benefits from any physical activity. Whatever physical activity you enjoy, try to engage in it on a regular basis. If the exercise is light, try to do it every day. If the exercise is more vigorous and aerobic, do it at least three times a week for 20 to 30 minutes. You may want to engage in a variety of different physical activities, to help keep you interested and motivated. Just be sure to keep to your routine. If you discontinue exercise, the benefits you have gained will quickly disappear.

What's the Best Way to Start an Exercise Program?   Because your heart and body will need time to get accustomed to any increase in physical activity, it's best to start slowly. You may want to start, for example, with 5 minutes of brisk walking a day. Then, after a week, you may want to add another 5 or 10 minutes, gradually building up to a half hour or 45 minutes of brisk walking. Similarly, if you are starting to run or jog, you may want to begin with 5 minutes of jogging or running, alternating it with walking. Then, as you become more fit, you can gradually build up to 20 minutes or a half hour of running.

For most people, the benefits of exercise outweigh any risks. If you are approaching forty or older, have serious health problems, or are at high risk for heart disease, be sure to check with your physician before starting too vigorous an exercise program.

Coping with Stress

In addition to the excellent benefits regular exercise offers your heart and health, it is also a terrific way to deal with stress. As we discussed in the previous chapter, stress is a significant risk factor for heart disease. My friend the surgeon-turned-ice-cream-salesman found a way to cope with the stress in his life by changing jobs and lifestyles. Yet how many of us are willing to quit our jobs just to reduce our stress?

Another answer to minimizing the negative impact of stress on our health is to use coping strategies, or simple methods for managing stress and anxiety. Certainly regular exercise is an excellent coping strategy. But what can you do when your boss suddenly blows up at you, or when you're stuck in traffic on your way to the movies? Whenever you feel uncomfortable with your level of stress—when you feel you can't control your emotions or behavior—you may want to try some stress-management techniques. The good news is that there are coping strategies so subtle that no one will know you're using them. Three effective, easy-to-learn techniques are listed below.

The Stress Log

This is a useful stress-management technique to start with because it helps you recognize your own stress, the source of it, and what action you can take to reduce it. The more you are aware and conscious of the stress, the more you can control its negative emotional impact. For one week keep a log of all the stress you experience. Using a notebook, set up one page for each day of the week and draw a chart. Across the top of each sheet, write down the following five column headings: "Time," "Stressor," "Physical Reaction," "Emotions," and "Plan." During the day, as you feel yourself stressed, fill out the chart (do not fill in the "Plan" column yet). For example, one entry might look like this:

> 5:00 P.M. Stuck in traffic. I have a tight feeling in my chest.
> I feel very angry and hostile.

Throughout the week, continue to note each stressful incident, no matter what it is, and add to your stress log. At the end of the week, after you've completed your log, flip back and read each entry. Under the column marked "Plan," write down a simple plan of action for lessening the severity of the situation. A good plan for the traffic example might be "Leave work 15 minutes earlier." Or, perhaps "Play relaxing music in my car." No matter what the situation is, you can come up with a means to help you feel more at ease and more in control.

Thought-Stopping

It's normal to be occasionally plagued by fears and worries. But excessive worry can be a source of constant stress. The following thought-stopping technique can prevent you from "stressing out" over issues such as mortgage or car payments.

Sit by yourself in a room where you won't be disturbed. For a couple of minutes, let yourself worry about anything that's on your mind. Allow yourself to totally concentrate on these unpleasant facts. After a moment, see a stop sign in your mind's eye and say the word *no* aloud. Then take a slow, deep breath and count to five. Look at something in the room or study your hand for a moment. Focus your attention on what you see. This should clear your mind of those stressful thoughts.

Once you've become familiar with thought-stopping, you can imagine hearing *no* without actually saying it. This allows you to control the stressful thoughts rather than letting them control you.

Meditation

Meditation is a potent method for relaxing tensed muscles and relieving the day's stresses. For centuries, practitioners of yoga and transcendental meditation have known this. Meditation also offers real physical benefits. A study conducted at the Harvard Medical School proved that meditation can lower an individual's blood pressure. All of us could stand to lessen the pressure against our arterial walls.

The technique is easy. Find a comfortable chair in a room where you won't be disturbed for at least 20 minutes. Then close your eyes and think of the number one. As you inhale slowly, say the number aloud or to yourself; then exhale. Imagine seeing nothing else but the number in front of you. Concentrate on it. Breathe in slowly and exhale slowly.

As you continue to breathe, you'll notice yourself growing more relaxed. Let yourself enjoy this, without letting anyone or anything disturb you. Your attention should still be on the number one; your breathing should be deep and regular.

When the 20 minutes are over, don't jerk yourself out of this relaxed state. Slowly, to a count of ten, bring yourself back to the present. Notice how refreshed and calm you feel.

Try these and other coping techniques until you determine which ones you're most comfortable with. Remember, the goal is to make them part of your everyday life in order to minimize the negative effects of stress.

An Ounce of Prevention

Everyone can benefit from the risk-reducing measures described in this chapter. If you've always wanted to quit smoking, now's the time to get some help and do it once and for all. If you've been worried about your diet, get the whole family involved and turn good health into a culinary adventure. And if your couch-potato conscience has been bothering you, find a friend who wants to start an exercise program and get going—it can be great fun!

Taking a few simple preventive steps now could mean an enormous savings in physical, emotional, and financial stress down the road. You *can* take control of your health—you *can* reduce your risk of heart disease!

5

Medications to Prevent Heart Disease

Cholesterol-Lowering Drugs

If after improving your diet, initiating a regular program of exercise, and quitting smoking, you still have a cholesterol count over 260, you need to talk to your physician about the possibility of taking medication. A variety of effective medications have come onto the market in recent years for the control of elevated cholesterol and other lipids (fats). This does not mean you should give up on your healthy regimen and replace it with medication; the drugs we outline in this chapter are meant to be an additional step, not an alternative path.

If you have been told you have a blood lipid abnormality, you may have one or more of a spectrum of disorders, all of which promote atherosclerosis. The most relevant of these disorders seems to involve cholesterol metabolism. However, other lipids such as triglycerides and phospholipids when abnormally elevated have also proven to be a factor in the development of atherosclerosis.

In the last few years, there has been a flurry of activity in the treatment of these disorders that has yielded promising results. A recent Veterans Administration report summarized these developments as follows (I describe these substances later on):

1. Colestipol-niacin controls elevated cholesterol and induces regression of coronary atherosclerosis.
2. Gemfibrozil or lovastatin stops the manufacturing of cholesterol in the body.
3. Gemfibrozil raises high-density lipoprotein (HDL) cholesterol levels.
4. The addition of small amounts of food rich in stearic or oleic acid makes a cholesterol-lowering regimen more palatable (these fatty acids are found in chicken and beef, soybeans, corn, and peanuts).

Doctors can prescribe any of the three drug regimens as treatment for high cholesterol, in addition to recommending dietary changes (including the consumption of stearic or oleic acid).

A Word on HDL. HDL is the fraction of the cholesterol equation that has been found to be the principal indicator of atherosclerotic risk, and it is called the HDL-C subfraction. People with high levels of HDL have a low level of coronary artery disease. If the HDL is low—even if the total cholesterol level is low—the incidence of coronary artery disease will be elevated. What this information indicates is that total cholesterol is important as an initial indicator of risk, but for real accuracy we need to know the level of the HDL. If the HDL level is low, it can be increased by weight reduction, aerobic exercise, cessation of smoking, consumption of foods high in monounsaturates, and, failing those, by such drugs as gemfibrozil or niacin.

Certainly it is optimal to have a high HDL. However, as I said earlier, we do not mean to imply that high HDL totally protects an individual from coronary artery disease.

A number of drugs have been developed to lower one or another of the various lipids in the bloodstream and thereby reduce atherosclerosis and coronary artery disease. Numerous studies have been done on thousands of patients over many years to substantiate the efficacy of these drugs, which again are only to be taken according to your doctor's prescription.

Cholestyramine (Questran). This drug lowers total cholesterol and low-density lipoproteins (LDL) and has been found to lower nonfatal heart attack rates by nearly 20 percent. It has also been found to have a mild effect on atherosclerotic regression. It is a resin that binds with bile acids (that are derived from cholesterol) and prevents their reabsorption. As a result they are excreted and the cholesterol level is lowered. Cholestyramine may cause constipation and abdominal distress. In addition, it may cause a depletion of fat-soluble vitamins, such as A, D, and K.

Gemfibrozil (Lopid). Gemfibrozil lowers LDL and elevates HDL-C. It also substantially reduces triglycerides. It was found to lower the incidence of nonfatal heart attacks by nearly 35 percent. The Food and Drug Administration (FDA) has approved it for the treatment of patients with low HDL, elevated LDL, or elevated triglyceride levels. Gemfibrozil may cause gastrointestinal problems and might possibly lead to gallbladder disease.

Niacin (Nicotinic Acid). Niacin has been found to reduce cholesterol by about 10 percent. In long-term studies it has substantially reduced the heart attack rate in people who had already had a first attack and reduced their mortality rate by 11 percent. It can have significant gastrointestinal and dermatologic side effects such as nausea, intestinal cramps, diarrhea, skin rashes, itching, flushing, headaches, and blurred vision. The use of niacin, like lovastatin (see below), requires that your liver be regularly monitored. As with other drugs listed here, use this powerful drug only under a doctor's supervision.

Colestipol (Colestid) Plus Niacin. This combination of drugs was used in patients who didn't smoke, did not have high blood pressure, and were on a low-fat diet but still had elevated cholesterol. The results were impressive. Total cholesterol was lowered 26 percent, LDL was reduced 43 percent, and HDL was elevated 37 percent. Interestingly, this drug combination has been shown to cause regression of coronary lesions by 16 percent and to reduce the overall progression of atherosclerosis. Colestipol may have the same side effects as cholestyramine (see above).

Probucol (Lorelco). The main benefit of probucol is the lowering of LDL by 10 percent. However, it also lowers HDL by about 25 percent. It seems to work by affecting cellular metabolism in the development of atherosclerotic lesions. Its side effects include gastrointestinal distress and arrhythmias.

Lovastatin (Mevacor). Lovastatin is one of a series of new drugs classified as "HMG-CoA reductase enzyme inhibitors." What this means is that lovastatin blocks the enzyme that is needed in the synthesis of LDL. As a result, LDL levels are substantially reduced by 30 to 40 percent. Triglycerides are also reduced 20 to 25 percent. HDL-C is increased by nearly 10 percent. This drug is more effective in lowering cholesterol than cholestyramine and has fewer side effects.

Oleic and Stearic Acids.   To make low-fat, low-cholesterol diets more palatable for patients requiring severe dietary restrictions, stearic and oleic acids are being added to the diets. Stearic acid is fully saturated and is found in cocoa butter, beef, and many animal fats. But it does not raise cholesterol. Oleic acid is nearly totally saturated, but similarly does not raise cholesterol. It is found in olive oil. Neither acid has an effect on HDL.

Combinations of these treatments are becoming the most popular approach to cholesterol problems. In fact, all the above-mentioned drugs have been or are being tested in combination. The advantage of this approach is to maximize the lipid-lowering effect of each of the drugs and to minimize the side effects they might have.

Antihypertensive Drugs

If you have developed a healthier diet, an exercise regimen, and have given up smoking, and yet your blood pressure remains above 160/95, your doctor may recommend antihypertensive drugs to bring it down. There are a wide variety of these drugs available, and sometimes more than one is needed. Not all of these drugs can be reviewed here, but we will review the more common types. These include beta-blockers, diuretics, calcium channel blockers, vasodilators, and ACE inhibitors.

Beta-Blockers.   Beta-blockers have been considered wonder drugs for the last twenty years. In fact in the mid-1970s, one of the first beta-blockers, Inderal, was also one of the most widely prescribed drugs in the world. Originally beta-blockers were used for the control of angina and to block the effect of hormones, such as noradrenaline, on the heart. Beta-blockers protect the heart from overstimulation and thereby lessen its workload. It was found that beta-blockers were effective in controlling hypertension as well as lowering the heart rate. The development of other beta-blocking drugs followed this discovery. Tenormin has been a popular prescription because it needs to be taken only once a day, compared with the more frequent dosages required of Inderal.

Diuretics.   These drugs act according to an entirely different mechanism. Used alone or in combination with other antihypertensive drugs, diuretics can lower blood pressure by reducing water volume and electrolytes (including sodium) by causing them to be excreted in the urine.

Calcium Channel Blockers.   Procardia and Nifedipine are examples of these drugs that block the entry of calcium into the heart cells. This keeps the heart from contracting vigorously. The heart muscle and the vascular system are, therefore, more relaxed and blood pressure is reduced. In some people, side effects of gastrointestinal distress, dizziness, or headaches can occur.

Vasodilators.   One class of vasodilators, alpha-blockers, has become widely used in recent years. These drugs block receptors, called alpha-receptors, on the blood vessels, allowing the vessels to dilate. This in effect reduces the vessels' resistance to blood flow, which lowers the blood pressure. These extremely potent drugs can reduce blood pressure within minutes when administered intravenously.

ACE Inhibitors. ACE (angiotensin converting enzyme) inhibitors are among the newest antihypertensive drugs. Captopril (Capoten) was the first of this new class of drugs. ACE inhibitors act by blocking the action of angiotensin, a potent hormone that elevates blood pressure. These drugs are useful for heart failure as well. Because they are very powerful drugs, caution is necessary when administering them. These drugs lower the output of blood from the heart; therefore, they may cause hypotension or dizziness and result in a temporarily accelerated heartbeat.

The wide variety of antihypertensive drugs gives a great deal of latitude to prescribing physicians. If when taking any blood pressure medication you experience unpleasant side effects, consult your doctor. The dosage of the drug may have to be changed or a different one prescribed.

Should You Take Aspirin?

In the early 1980s, studies showed aspirin to be effective in preventing second heart attacks, reducing the incidence by about 20 percent. Since then numerous reports have come from all over the world either substantiating or refuting the efficacy of aspirin when used alone or in combination with some other drug, such as dipyridamole (Persantine). For example, in a 1988 study of 22,000 U.S. physicians over the age of forty, it was found that the incidence of all heart attacks fell by over a third, and fatal heart attacks dropped by more than half when the doctors took one aspirin tablet (325 milligrams) every other day.

In contrast, a British study of 7,000 subjects compared the

incidence of heart disease among those who took 500 milligrams of aspirin daily—a dosage three times greater than in the U.S. study—and among those who took no aspirin. The British study found no relationship between daily aspirin intake and the incidence of heart attacks. Currently, most experts suggest there are benefits to taking aspirin on a once-a-day or once-every-other-day basis. But the benefits are limited, as far as we presently know, and probably fall somewhere in between the two above-mentioned studies.

Aspirin studies are ongoing and are always being refined. Limitations to some of the reports, including the ones listed here, were that the participants were healthy to begin with, had a low incidence of hypertension, and had low cholesterol levels. Furthermore few of the subjects smoked. Regular aspirin taking in populations with preexisting heart disease might have a different effect than it did in these low-risk groups. Although researchers think the results would probably be similar among women, most of the subjects in this U.S. study were men, making conclusions speculative.

But aspirin does have certain identifiable effects. Unlike other pain relievers, such as ibuprofen and acetaminophen, aspirin inhibits the clotting of blood. Because it makes the blood thinner and stops platelet accumulation, aspirin has certain preventive powers. For example, it has been shown to decrease the incidence of strokes in people with blockages in the arteries to the brain. It is also prescribed after balloon angioplasty procedures. Unfortunately, taking an aspirin daily or every other day brings with it certain problems. Because aspirin affects your blood platelets and thus inhibits clotting, it may increase your tendency to bleed. In addition, aspirin can cause internal bleeding or irritation of the stomach. Moreover, some people are overtly allergic to it.

Like other drugs, aspirin is not a cure-all. It also has no effect on the other risk factors for vascular disease: it does absolutely nothing to rid the body of cholesterol and other fats or to prevent the accumulation of fatty plaque on the blood vessel wall. So don't use aspirin or any other drug as a substitute for quitting smoking, improving your diet, or building a healthy program of exercise. The final word on aspirin has yet to be uttered. Use it judiciously and only after consulting your physician about dosage.

6

Recognizing the Symptoms
of Heart Disease

So far, this book has concentrated on factors that contribute to the development of heart disease and the control of those factors. And if you follow these recommendations closely, this chapter will probably be unnecessary. However, it is important, especially because some of you may be at high risk, that you know the signs of heart disease—for both you and your family members. What does it feel like to have angina (chest pain)? What are the early warning signs of a heart attack? After reading this section you'll be better prepared to recognize the signals the body may at some point give you or someone you love. Figures 3 and 4 are diagrams of the heart to guide you through this chapter.

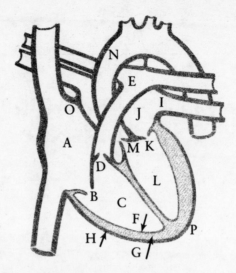

Figure 3. Cross section of the heart. A. Right atrium, B. tricuspid valve, C. right ventricle, D. pulmonary valve, E. pulmonary artery, F. endocardium, G. myocardium, H. epicardium, I. pulmonary vein, J. left atrium, K. mitral valve, L. left ventricle, M. aortic valve, N. aorta, O. sinus node; and P. apex.
Courtesy of American Heart Association /New York City Affiliate.

How the Heart Works

The average heart beats 100,000 times in a single day, pumping more than 2,000 gallons of blood throughout the body's circulatory system. With a series of smooth, measured, rhythmic contractions, the heart pumps blood regularly and efficiently to the various organs and extremities of the body. We give the heart a greater workout than any other muscle in the body, contracting and relaxing it from 2.5 to 3.5 billion times in the course of an average lifetime.

Blood flows into the heart's two collecting chambers, the

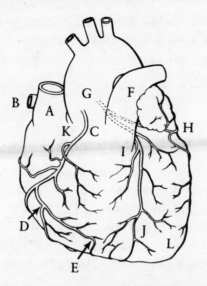

Figure 4. Anterior view of the heart. A. Superior vena cava; B. right pulmonary artery; C. right coronary artery; D. posterior descending branch, right coronary artery; E. marginal branch, right coronary artery; F. left pulmonary artery; G. left coronary artery; H. circumflex branch, left coronary artery; I. anterior descending branch, left coronary artery, J. marginal branch, left coronary artery, K. sinus node; and L. apex.
Courtesy of American Heart Association/New York City Affiliate.

atria. The right atrium gathers oxygen-depleted blood from the body and pumps it into the right ventricle. This ventricle then pumps the blood through the pulmonary artery to the lungs, which reinfuse it with oxygen. Oxygen-rich blood traveling from the lungs collects in the left atrium and then passes into the left ventricle, which pumps it through the aorta (the main blood vessel leading from the heart) to the rest of the body. About 5 percent of the blood pumped by the left ventricle goes to feed the heart muscle itself, which uses more oxygen than any other part of the body.

Blood feeds the heart muscle by flowing into the first two

branches that leave the aorta, the coronary arteries. These main blood vessels provide the heart with blood, rich in both the oxygen and nutrients it needs to operate regularly and efficiently.

How the Heart Stops Working

Unlike some diseases, coronary disease progresses gradually. As you have seen, a combination of poor diet, lack of exercise, cigarette smoking, and other unhealthy habits—in addition to genetic factors—inflict their damage day by day over the course of many years. And it is the slow progressive nature of the disease that gives you the power to take positive action to prevent or delay it.

As we have already illustrated, atherosclerosis results from the progressive accumulation of fat and cholesterol deposits on arterial walls, a process similar to the way mineral deposits or corrosion collect on the inside of a water pipe. And just as mineral deposits or corrosion can end up choking the supply of water to your house, this accumulation of fatty plaque deposits can clog the blood vessel, blocking the supply of blood to the heart. Coronary heart disease and vascular disease elsewhere in the body result whenever atherosclerosis narrows an artery to such an extent that it can no longer supply sufficient blood and oxygen to meet the needs of the body. This disparity between supply and demand can become especially severe during times of physical or emotional stress, when the heart's demand for oxygen increases dramatically.

This impediment to the flow of blood is seldom noticeable until approximately one-half of the blood vessel is blocked. In many cases, even with significant blockages, the resulting ischemia (insufficient supply of blood) goes totally unnoticed. An estimated 2 million Americans suffer from what is called silent ischemia, which remains undetected unless and until the sufferer comes to the hospital with a heart attack. Despite the reduced flow of blood to the heart muscle, silent ischemia produces no pain whatsoever. Because the lack of symptoms allows it to go undetected for so long, damage to the heart muscle can be significant. Pain that occurs with ischemia is called angina, described below.

An additional 2 to 3 million Americans suffer from angina. Angina, a temporary pressure pain in the chest, arms, or jaw, is brought on when the muscle of the heart gets less oxygen than it needs due to artery blockage or spasm. But unlike a cramp in a muscle of an arm or leg, you can't rest the heart. It continues to beat, and with each contraction, starving for oxygen, the heart sends out signals of distress through nerve pathways. If the pain comes on at a point of increased physical activity—such as walking up steps—stopping that activity and giving the heart a moment to slow down and lessen its demand for oxygen will decrease anginal pain.

Many angina sufferers point to smoking, exercise after a heavy meal, walking, sex, and getting up in the morning as common physical activities that precede angina attacks. The frequency of these attacks varies from patient to patient and can occur many times during the day or only a few times during the year. Angina is often the first clue people have that something is wrong with their heart, and it brings many people into doctors' offices for treatment.

When an obstruction in the coronary artery does more than merely restrict the flow of blood, going so far as to totally choke off the passageway, the acute shortage of oxygen-rich blood results in a heart attack . . . known as a myocardial infarction. This total blockage may result from atherosclerosis alone, from a spasm in the artery, or from a blood clot lodged in the atherosclerotic vessel. Whatever the immediate cause of the blockage, however, the part of the heart muscle normally supplied with blood through that coronary artery becomes seriously starved of oxygen.

Smaller arteries that serve heart tissue near the blocked coronary artery may try to take up some of the slack. But these collateral vessels can only provide up to 40 percent of the blood the main coronary artery should carry. Often this is enough to avoid permanent damage. But just as often it is not enough, and the heart damage is permanent. If a great deal of heart muscle is affected, the victim of a heart attack may die.

The heart muscle may sustain so much damage from a heart attack that heart failure results. Heart failure, more properly called congestive heart failure, does not mean that the heart has stopped, but simply that its functioning has been seriously impaired. Of course, there are all degrees of heart failure from mild to nearly terminal. The mild type can usually be controlled with medications. Patients with the end stage, terminal type have very little functioning heart muscle and require a heart transplant if they are to survive.

Sudden cardiac death results from the complications of a heart attack. In a healthy individual, the heart's natural pacemaker, the sinus node, controls the heartbeat by discharging electrical impulses that travel to the heart muscle and cause it to contract. A heart attack may cause the heart's electrical system to "short-circuit," producing serious irregularities in the beating of the heart, called arrhythmias. Cardiac arrhythmias can take several forms: the heart may occasionally skip a beat; it may beat extremely rapidly, an arrhythmia known as tachycardia; it may beat extremely slowly, an arrhythmia known as bradycardia; or it may twitch haphazardly and ineffectively, an arrhythmia known as fibrillation. In healthy people, some arrhythmias may arise as a normal response to exercise or stress and occur in about 5 percent of people who don't have coronary disease, producing no known detrimental consequences. In heart attack patients, however, arrhythmias can be serious.

The most serious arrhythmias that commonly occur in the hours following a heart attack are ventricular tachycardia and ventricular fibrillation. When ventricular tachycardia lasts for more than a few seconds, the volume of blood pumped by the heart decreases sharply, leaving the victim short of breath, dizzy, and faint, and possibly sending him into shock. Ultimately, ventricular tachycardia can worsen into ventricular fibrillation, the most serious type of cardiac arrhythmia, in which effective functioning of the heart ceases entirely. This is an emergency and requires cardiopulmonary resuscitation (CPR).

During fibrillation, the heart's rhythm completely degenerates, resulting in an uncoordinated flurry of electrical impulses in the left ventricle. These random electrical charges cause the heart to twitch uselessly, halting regular heartbeats and the pumping of blood. Unless proper functioning of the heart is restored quickly with CPR, the victim of ventricular fibrillation will die.

Recognizing the Warning Signs of Heart Disease

The key to surviving a heart attack is to recognize the warning signs promptly and get immediate medical attention. Heart attack victims who make it to a hospital have a reasonable survival rate. However, of the 540,000 annual heart attack deaths in the United States, more than 300,000 occur *before* the victim reaches the hospital. This happens despite the fact that the first signs of a heart attack often occur as much as 3 to 4 hours prior to cardiac death. Those who have suffered heart attacks have described this intense pain—which results from the heart trying to pump even though it lacks sufficient oxygen—as crushing, heavy pressure, or as a smothering or choking feeling. It has also been described as feeling like a truck is being parked on the chest or the heart is being squeezed by a vise. Angina pain is the most common sign of an ensuing heart attack, although it does not necessarily mean one is about to happen. Angina can first manifest just prior to a heart attack or can be present for months as a warning sign, getting worse just preceding an attack.

Because the tightness in the chest may be relatively mild, many heart attack victims who are unaware of their infliction or do not wish to acknowledge the cause of their pain mistake this discomfort for nothing more than severe indigestion. It is common to relegate the cause of chest pain to an over-worked stomach, particularly after a heavy meal. If you or a loved one experience chest pain—no matter how mild—that matches the description above, be sure to see a doctor immediately.

Many patients who have a sharp pain in their chest think they are having a heart attack. But if the pain is sharp, its cause is usually something else, such as costochondritis, an inflammation of the rib where it joins with the cartilage, or a pain from the gastrointestinal tract. However, when in doubt, again, consult your doctor.

You should be aware that angina discomfort may not re-main localized in the area of the chest. It can spread, radiating to the jaw, neck, or throat, to the left or right arms, to the shoulders or back.

Most people mistakenly think chest pain is the *only* indication of heart disease. But a heart attack can also manifest itself in other ways. More than half of those who suffer heart attacks complain of nausea and vomiting. Others describe feeling unusually weak, dizzy, or faint. If you suffer a heart attack, you may notice heart palpitations or irregularities in your heartbeat. Or you might feel short of breath, experience numbness in your fingers, and/or break out in a cold sweat. Consult a doctor immediately.

So, as you can see, an entire spectrum of symptoms of heart disease exists, from silent ischemia to crushing pains to fatal arrhythmias. Being aware of them is crucial for those of us with heart disease in our families.

What to Do If You Suspect You're Having a Heart Attack

IF YOU FEEL ANY CHEST DISCOMFORT THAT LASTS FOR MORE THAN 2 MINUTES OR ANY COMBINATION OF THE OTHER SYMPTOMS, SEEK MEDICAL ATTENTION QUICKLY.

The average delay between the onset of symptoms and obtaining professional care—2 to 4 hours—may make the difference between life and death. Most victims tend to react with strong protests of denial: "This can't be happening to me!" Don't waste time fooling yourself in this way. And be sure to ask for the help of those around you: You should not drive when experiencing chest pain.

A Brief Test on the Warning Signs
of Heart Attack and What to Do

Because quick recognition of the warning signs could end up saving your or your family member's life, it is important to learn them. Moreover, if a heart attack strikes, you need to know what to do. Take this quick quiz to make sure you understand this information.

Questions

1. True or False? All victims of heart attacks feel intense pain in their chest. _____
2. Name five sensations that could be warning signs of heart attack. _____
   _____
   _____
   _____
   _____
3. True or False? If you feel any of the warning signs of a heart attack, you should wait for an hour or so to see if they go away. _____
4. True or False? If you think you are having a heart attack, you should drive to the hospital immediately. _____
5. True or False? Your chances of surviving heart disease are better if someone in your family has been trained in CPR. _____

Answers

1. False. Some heart attack victims feel milder discomfort while others feel no pain at all.

2. Any of the following may warn you of a heart attack:
   - Intense chest pain: crushing, smothering, pressurelike.
   - More moderate chest pain: tightness, pressure, vague discomfort.
   - Pain that radiates from the chest to the arms, throat, jaw, shoulder, or back.
   - Shortness of breath.
   - Nausea and/or vomiting.
   - Unusual weakness.
   - Dizziness or faintness.
   - Heart palpitations or arrhythmias.
   - Numbness in fingers.
   - Breaking into a cold sweat.
3. False. Get immediate medical care. Do not delay, hoping that the symptoms will go away.
4. False. You should get to a hospital immediately, but because a heart attack can cause unconsciousness, you should not drive yourself.
5. True.

The Importance of Diagnostic Tests

If you or a family member suffers a heart attack or are diagnosed as having angina, when the immediate crisis is over one or more tests will be necessary. Some of these tests are done routinely during a checkup. Others are done on an acute, or emergency, basis. For example, if a heart attack is suspected, when you get to the hospital your blood samples will be analyzed for the presence of certain enzymes that escape into the bloodstream when a portion of the heart is injured. The results of this test will help confirm your cardiologist's diagnosis of myocardial infarction (heart attack). In addition, other tests now exist that can check for signs of heart disease as well as measuring the extent of the disease.

If you have three or more high-risk factors for coronary heart disease, and no matter your age, you should consult your physician about taking some of these tests even if you *haven't* suffered from an attack of angina, a heart attack, or some other problem. Since silent ischemia strikes without revealing itself, you or other family members may already have suffered some of the affects of coronary heart disease without even knowing it. An early warning may help you and your physician take measures to keep your heart disease under control.

Electrocardiogram

The most common test of heart activity is the electrocardiogram (ECG or EKG). It is performed more than 21 million times a year in the United States. The ECG will measure, amplify, and record the heart's electrical activity during the few minutes it takes to perform the procedure. It does so through electrodes that are attached to the wrists, ankles, and chest. It measures the heart's activity when at rest. Besides helping to recognize arrhythmias, an ECG can detect if any damage has been done to the heart muscle. The test is usually done in a doctor's office, a hospital, or a commercial lab.

Exercise Stress Test

Because a regular ECG only records your heart's resting electrical activity, your physician may want you to undergo an exercise stress test, also called an exercise electrocardiogram. The purpose of this test is to exercise the heart and increase its demand for blood and oxygen. The exercise stress test may reveal signs of blockage, such as silent ischemia or arrhythmias, that might be apparent only in response to stress, in this case the strain of physical activity. This test might actually precipitate angina. Commonly, people with coronary artery disease will develop chest pain, shortness of breath, or fatigue early on in the test. But others with significant disease may have no symptoms. In either case, the ECG that is being recorded will show the heart's abnormalities. Thus the stress test can tip you off to the presence of otherwise undetected atherosclerosis in the coronary arteries. This is one reason why doctors often recommend it before prescribing a regimen of strenuous physical activity (and why people at high risk should consult their physicians before starting an exercise program).

To participate in this test you walk (or jog) on a treadmill or ride a stationary bicycle. Whichever machine you use, it will be designed to raise your heart rate gradually until you reach a predetermined target rate. The treadmill progressively becomes more strenuous by speeding up gradually, simulating a greater upward slant. While you exercise, a nurse or lab technician will regularly check your blood pressure and pulse and an electrocardiogram will record your heart's activity. Expect to feel a bit tired, slightly breathless, and sweaty by the end of the test. The medical staff will then continue to monitor your pulse, blood pressure, and heart rhythms for 10 to 15 minutes after you get off the treadmill. A bicycle test is conducted in the same manner.

The stress test is performed on asymptomatic people (individuals with no symptoms) on a periodic basis after the age of forty. For individuals who exercise and are in good cardiovascular condition the stress test will be uneventful. However, for people who don't exercise or who have cardiovascular problems, the stress test will be tiring.

If you have symptoms of angina, the stress test is performed to evaluate how long you can exercise and how rapid your heart will beat before abnormalities occur in the ECG. If the stress test remains normal, then your chest pains are probably not angina. As soon as the test does become abnormal, or if angina or excess shortness of breath develops, the physician will stop the test and note how many minutes you were able to exercise.

If a stress test determines that there is blockage in the coronary arteries, your doctor will probably recommend further tests—such as a cardiac catheterization—to identify precisely the extent and location of the blockage (this test is discussed later in this chapter).

The Holter Monitor

The Holter monitor is a portable, battery-operated electrocardiogram. It provides a continuous 24-hour monitor of the heart's electrical activity as a person goes through his daily activities. It is used mostly to detect arrhythmias. Like the exercise stress test, the Holter monitor, which records the heart's activity under a variety of conditions, can provide a more accurate indication of coronary heart disease than the standard ECG test, which only monitors the heart's activity while at rest.

The Holter monitor is usually set up in your doctor's office. Electrodes are attached to the skin of your chest, and then you are instructed to continue on with your daily activities. A shoulder strap or belt holds a small tape recorder that will record your heart's activity over the next 24 hours. The newer machines are remarkably small and should not interfere with your normal activities. You must write down the exact times and nature of all of your daily activities in a diary or notebook. Such a list would include waking, sleeping, working, exercising, sex, emotional disturbances, etc. If an irregularity shows up on the Holter monitor, you will be able to look in your diary to see what you were doing when it occurred and report to your doctor.

Echocardiogram

An echocardiogram uses extremely high frequency (ultrasonic) sound waves to create pictures of the heart in action. These images can be used to detect abnormalities in the heart's chambers and measure their size. An echocardiogram can also help detect valve disease or other indications of coronary heart disease.

An echocardiogram works in roughly the same way that sonar helps a submarine navigate, employing sound waves to detect the presence and shape of objects in its path. First, a technician places a transducer on your chest. This device emits an ultrasound beam of inaudible sound waves, which is aimed toward the heart chambers and valves. The transducer needs to remain in contact with the skin because it not only sends out the ultrasound beams, but also picks them up as they bounce back. During the test the technician will change the angle of the transducer several times and ask you to shift your position as well. In this way all the different areas of the heart can be examined. The images of the heart are projected on a monitor and recorded on videotape, offering an accurate assessment of the organ's functioning.

Thallium Imaging

Thallium imaging, also known as thallium scintigraphy, also provides images of the heart in action, but it creates these pictures by nuclear scanning rather than by ultrasonic waves. Thallium imaging traces the course of blood as it travels through your heart. It can detect normal or abnormal heart function depending on the amount of thallium distributed throughout the heart muscle.

A small amount of this safe radioactive substance is injected into a vein in your arm. The technician who performs this test will ask you to change positions as a scanner follows the progression of thallium through the heart. The scintillation camera converts the radioactive reading into colored images, which are displayed and recorded on a video screen. The various colors that are displayed indicate how much thallium has been taken up by various parts of the heart muscle. For example, a normal area of the heart will be displayed as red. An area of the heart not receiving sufficient blood will be displayed as blue. A spectrum of colors in between may also show up and will vary as the heart beats. This test can be performed while at rest or with exercise.

Cardiac Catheterization and Angiography

This test is usually only given to patients who have undergone some of the previously mentioned screening tests. If coronary artery disease is suspected after the other evaluations, then cardiac catheterization and angiography is done to evaluate the necessity for corrective procedures such as balloon angioplasty or surgery. (Most hospitals report that only about one-third of patients who receive cardiac catheterization and angiography will require balloon angioplasty or surgery.) This procedure is discussed last because the other screening tests are noninvasive (that is, no catheters or instruments enter the body), less expensive, and prevent many patients without serious symptoms from undergoing the more extensive testing.

If you do need a cardiac catheterization and angiography, the following explanation will give you a general idea of the procedure: A small, flexible catheter is inserted into either a large artery in your groin (the femoral artery) or an artery in your arm (the brachial artery) after the area has been anesthetized. The catheter is then threaded up the artery until it reaches your heart. All the time the journey of the catheter is observed under video control. You may even be able to watch on a monitor as the procedure is done, but you won't feel the catheter move through your body. This is the part of the procedure known as catheterization. In the angiography part of the procedure, dye is injected through the catheter to help highlight the chambers of the heart and the coronary arteries. You will then receive a series of injections that will determine the status of the arteries from different angles. It often takes a number of views to determine the presence of blockage and the degree of obstruction. With these injections, the cardiologist can follow the progress of the dye through the arteries and pinpoint the location of arterial blockages, spasm, or other pathology.

Tests like these provide patients and doctors with valuable tools for detecting heart disease. Heart disease is usually treatable. If your tests come up positive, there's plenty you and your doctor can do to fight back. The next chapter outlines the treatments at your disposal and your outlook for recovery.

7

If You Develop Heart Disease...
A Promising Outlook
for Recovery

This chapter is designed to give you some idea of what treatments are available should you or a loved one develop heart disease. It is meant to be reassuring and educational, not frightening. Neither you nor a loved one may ever need these treatments. But should you have a personal history or a significant family history of heart disease, you may find this chapter contains vital information for you and/or your family members.

The treatments for heart disease range from the simple to the sublime. As we explained earlier, coronary heart disease ranges in severity from no symptoms, to mild angina, to an uncomplicated heart attack, to a heart attack complicated with arrhythmias or heart failure. The treatments available provide a corresponding menu of choices depending on what degree of cardiac disease has developed. They range from drugs for angina, to "clot busters" for the acute heart attack, to heart transplantation. This chapter should demystify these treatments and allay concerns you may have regarding drugs or surgery.

The treatment of angina, heart attacks, heart failure, and ventricular fibrillation (a form of arrhythmia) has improved dramatically in the last twenty-five years. Revolutionary new drugs can destroy blood clots and limit the damage of a heart attack. And other new drug treatments as well as lasers and surgery can halt many arrhythmias. Balloon angioplasty can dilate some of the atherosclerotic lesions blocking the arteries and enable some patients to avoid surgery altogether. Lasers and atherectomy can also obviate the need for surgery by unblocking arteries. Moreover, bypass surgery is now performed safely and routinely on hundreds of thousands of patients annually. All these advances, and more yet to come, dramatically improve the chances of survival for affected patients and give them the promise of a normal and long life.

How to Halt an Angina Attack

Angina can usually be controlled relatively easily. In many cases, you can bring an angina attack to a halt simply by stopping the activity that brought on the episode. If you have regular episodes of angina, your physician will probably prescribe a drug called nitroglycerin, a powerful vasodilator (dilator of blood vessels). Although it can occasionally cause headaches or dizziness, nitroglycerin and other nitrates can quickly lower your blood pressure and decrease your heart's demand for oxygen. By dilating the arteries and smaller blood vessels that nourish the heart, nitroglycerin improves the flow of blood and increases the oxygen supply. By placing a nitroglycerin tablet under your tongue, you can relieve angina quickly.

If you suffer from frequent episodes of angina, you may need longer-acting nitrates. Nitroglycerin patches, now worn by over 1 million Americans, have proved extremely effective in controlling angina. Attached to the chest like an adhesive bandage, these patches administer a steady, uninterrupted dose of nitroglycerin, which is absorbed into the bloodstream through the skin. Although most manufacturers' labels suggest that you wear them constantly, studies have shown that nitroglycerin patches work best when worn for only 12 to 14 hours per day; this prevents your body from building up a tolerance to the drug. However, some patients must wear them constantly, so you should follow your physician's recommendation.

Most of the other drugs used to treat angina were described in "Antihypertensive Drugs," in chapter 5. In addition to vasodilators such as nitroglycerin, beta-blockers and calcium channel blockers are effective in treating angina. Besides lowering blood pressure, beta-blockers slow the heart rate, reduce the heart's demand for oxygen, and thus relieve anginal pain. Similarly, calcium channel blockers, which reduce blood pressure, can also reduce anginal pain. More and more frequently, beta-blockers and calcium channel blockers are being used in the treatment of angina, often in combination with nitroglycerin or as a replacement for it.

Naturally, whatever drug treatment you receive to manage your angina, you must also make changes in your lifestyle as recommended by your physician and described in chapter 4.

How to Stop a Heart Attack:
"Clot Busters"

Like angina, heart attacks can usually be treated with drug therapy, in combination with an aftercare program that involves an improved diet, an exercise plan, and kicking the smoking habit, if you have one. If you do suffer a heart attack, the first order of business is to stop the attack by eliminating the obstruction of your coronary arteries. This can now be done with the exciting advent of rapid clot dissolvers known as "clot busters."

These intravenously injected drugs act quickly and can completely dissolve an obstructing blood clot—within just a few minutes! Once a patient arrives at the hospital and is diagnosed with a heart attack, he may well receive one of these clot busters. If it is administered within the first 3 or 4 hours of the onset of an attack, it can actually stop a heart attack in progress and improve the chances of recovery by limiting the amount of irreversible damage done to the heart muscle.

This drug has proven so effective in some cases that it has been suggested that in the future it be given to patients by the paramedics instead of waiting until the patient arrives at the hospital. It is conceivable that someday a clot buster will be computer designed, synthetically bioengineered, and orally administered to dissolve blood clots as soon as a doctor suspects one is present.

The three clot buster drugs currently used are Urokinase, Streptokinase, and t-PA. Urokinase is rarely used for coronary clots, but is used extensively for blood clots in the peripheral arteries, such as in the leg. Streptokinase is an enzyme derived from the bacteria *Streptococcus,* an enzyme that is effective in causing the breakdown of certain chemical bonds that hold a clot together. In contrast, t-PA (tissue plasminogen activator) belongs to a new class of drugs that are genetically engineered—and are the result of fabulous imagination and scientific thinking. t-PA has been used successfully worldwide on many people to free obstructed arteries from the shackles of blood clots.

There is one side effect of these drugs. The current generation of genetically engineered clot busters, as well as Streptokinase and Urokinase, affects the clotting mechanisms of the *entire* body, not just the problem artery, and as a result can cause bleeding. This side effect is not common, but, for example, in the few minutes it takes for t-PA to wear off, bleeding has been noted to occur in the brain, the gastrointestinal tract, and elsewhere in the body where a susceptibility to bleeding may be present. As a result, this drug needs to be administered judiciously and under close supervision.

These clot busters are very effective treatments of the immediate problem: they stop a heart attack in progress and offer damage control. However, they do nothing to treat the more fundamental, underlying cause of heart attack: the coronary artery blockage. Even after the clot is destroyed, the artery remains narrowed due to atherosclerosis. This obstruction can continue to cause symptoms of angina and even a subsequent heart attack. After discontinuing the use of clot buster drugs, more than 20 percent of patients have a second heart attack. And of course, clot busters can do nothing to repair the damage done to the heart muscle caused by heart attack.

Depending on the medical status of the patient, various avenues can be taken after the initial clot busting treatment. The patient will be initially monitored in the intensive care unit (ICU). If there are no further signs of danger, the patient can sometimes go home within a few days. However, if the patient develops arrhythmias or heart failure, he will need additional hospitalization and treatment. In either case, many patients who suffer a heart attack will be given a cardiac catheterization so that the doctor can precisely visualize the obstructed coronary arteries. Some of those patients will undergo balloon angioplasty and/or coronary bypass surgery to repair the damage.

Correcting Arrhythmias

As we explained in chapter 6, recovering heart attack patients run the risk of developing potentially fatal arrhythmias, especially during the first hours and days after the attack. In addition, 15 percent of all hospitalized heart attack victims suffer a second attack while still in the hospital. To minimize these possibilities, the patient is initially placed in the ICU or coronary care unit (CCU) for close ECG monitoring.

If monitoring reveals arrhythmias, drugs will be administered to control them. Lidocaine, digitalis, verapamil (a calcium channel blocker), and Inderal (a beta-blocker) are among the more commonly used drugs. However, there is a panoply of other drugs for general or specific arrhythmia treatment.

Two particularly dangerous arrhythmias are treated with electronic devices. Bradycardia is when the heart beats too slowly for a period of time. For patients with this condition, it may become crucial to increase their heart rate to prevent the heart from stopping altogether. In this case, a pacemaker—a small, battery-powered device implanted under the skin of the chest—is used to control the heart rate.

The pacemaker is placed in the heart by a relatively simple procedure. Over the last twenty years, the electronics revolution has made pacemakers as small as a silver dollar, an astonishing fact when you consider that it contains enough sophisticated circuitry to control all sorts of rhythm disturbances and to respond to the patient's own body physiology. The current generation of pacers can increase the heart rate as a person exercises. Minimum and maximum rates can be programmed into the pacer to control specific arrhythmias and to allow the heart to function within a normal range.

The second dangerous arrhythmia is ventricular fibrillation, which consists of rapid, irregular heartbeats. If this life-threatening complication occurs, cardiopulmonary resuscitation (CPR) is needed. One method used is called defibrillation, which is commonly featured in emergency room scenes of movie and television shows to heighten drama. For this procedure, two metallic paddles are applied to the chest, sending a jolt of electricity directly to the heart. This electric shock disrupts the dangerous and ineffective electrical activity of the heart during fibrillation. It actually stops the heart momentarily to allow it to return to a normal heartbeat. Electric defibrillators, first used in the mid-1960s, can be remarkably effective, but must be applied immediately. Otherwise this arrhythmia will cause death.

If You Need Surgery

If you are diagnosed as having angina or a heart attack, your cardiologist will probably put you through certain tests after your condition has stabilized to assess the degree of damage. If the tests show narrowing and partial obstruction in just one coronary artery, your cardiologist may prescribe nothing more than drug therapy, dietary restrictions, and exercise. If the tests demonstrate blockage or severe narrowing in two or three of your primary coronary arteries, surgery may be recommended. Naturally, other factors will also play a part in that decision, including the extent of damage sustained by your heart muscle and your overall health. But in general, the more advanced your coronary atherosclerosis, the greater the likelihood that your treatment will involve surgery or balloon angioplasty.

Angioplasty (PTCA)

In the last decade, angioplasty has become an increasingly common treatment for narrowed coronary arteries. Cardiologists performed this procedure, more properly called "percutaneous transluminal coronary angioplasty," or PTCA, more than 200,000 times in 1988, a 50 percent increase from the total in 1986 and almost five times the number performed in 1984. Although it can cause complications, including injury to the blood vessels and possibly an actual heart attack, the incidence of complications has dropped and the success rates have climbed since the procedure was first performed.

Despite increasing effectiveness, some say angioplasty has become dangerously overused. A 1989 study by the National Heart, Lung and Blood Institute found that angioplasty was not necessary in many cases and should not be regarded as a routine procedure following a heart attack. A more conservative approach relying primarily on clot busters followed by aspirin and/or exercise showed comparable results in some studies.

Why the second thoughts about angioplasty? Because there is a significant failure rate. Many studies have shown that in less than six months, 20 to 40 percent of patients who underwent angioplasty showed reblockage in their coronary arteries and up to 10 percent suffered a second heart attack. The mortality of patients with failed angioplasty is significantly higher than in patients who go directly to surgery and are not given PTCA. Many patients want to avoid surgery and hope for a successful angioplasty, but if it fails they are often worse off than they were before the procedure.

Angioplasty begins with a cardiac catheterization. The cardiologist threads a small catheter into the blocked coronary artery. A tiny metal guide wire that can pass the obstruction is fed through that catheter. A tiny balloon catheter is fed over the guide wire and is positioned, under X-ray control, at the point of the obstruction. The balloon is then inflated. This sudden inflation, which lasts about 30 seconds, will flatten soft atherosclerotic plaque deposits against the arterial wall and widen the opening of the artery. Dye will be injected through the catheter, and an angiogram will be taken to check the effectiveness of the inflation procedure. Three or more inflations are commonly performed at each blockage site.

When successful, this technique results in a smoother, wider pathway restoring normal blood flow to a hungry muscle. After a recovery period of just one or two days in the hospital, the patient can usually go home, and he can often resume normal activities in about a week. Aspirin is commonly prescribed to minimize subsequent clotting episodes. While aspirin has been found to be effective after balloon angioplasty, its use as a preventive drug for coronary events is still controversial.

If reocclusion occurs, a second angioplasty may be attempted or surgery may be recommended.

Coronary Bypass Surgery

Throughout the 1980s and into the 1990s bypass surgery has been the most frequent type of heart surgery performed. In 1988, for example, there were 230,000 bypass surgeries, bringing the total number over the 2 million mark since the procedure was introduced in the late 1960s.

For patients with symptoms of advanced coronary disease, coronary bypass is effective in preventing a first or subsequent heart attack. This surgery is recommended if, despite drug therapy and lifestyle changes, the severity of angina restricts normal activities and work. There are many factors involved in patient selection for bypass surgery. Age, sex, and the presence of diabetes or hypertension are rarely contraindications. However, if the patient doesn't smoke, has a normal cholesterol level, and has not suffered serious heart muscle damage, the chances are much better that surgery will not be necessary. The coronary angiogram is first done to determine if a patient is a good candidate for surgery. If the main coronary artery is severely blocked, a dangerous condition that can prove fatal, surgery is almost always a must. If two or three of the coronary vessels are blocked, surgery is also necessary.

In a coronary bypass operation, surgeons construct new routes for blood that literally bypass the blocked sections of the heart's blood vessels. When the arteries that supply blood to the heart are blocked, the heart muscle does not get the oxygen it needs, and a heart attack can result. The new blood vessels created during coronary bypass surgery circumvent the blocked ones and direct blood to the areas of the heart previously deprived of blood. The heart can then function normally.

As with normal vessels, the bypass grafts can develop atherosclerosis over a period of time; however, the incidence of disease developing in these bypass grafts is significantly lower in patients with low cholesterol and in nonsmokers, another reason to minimize these risk factors. It has also been fairly well proven that bypass grafts stay open longer in patients with lower cholesterol levels.

Coronary bypass surgery is a major procedure, but it is also the most common and successful heart operation performed today. Just before surgery, the anesthesiologist will administer general anesthesia to the patient. The surgeon will then harvest a vein from the leg and, commonly, the internal mammary artery from under the chest wall. He or she will sew the graft into the blocked coronary arteries, beyond the obstructed section. This allows the flow of blood to go around the blocked areas. (If atherosclerosis has clogged more than one artery, your surgeon will use more than one graft, bypassing all blocked arteries. These operations are, therefore, called double bypasses or triple bypasses.)

A bypass patient stays in the hospital for about a week following the operation. The first few days are spent in the ICU where he is monitored for any problems and receives blood transfusions if necessary. Usually on the third postoperative day the patient is transferred to the intermediate care unit. There, while his heart activity is still monitored, the patient will begin walking, exercising, and gradually preparing to return home.

Coronary bypass operations do carry certain risks. They range from intraoperative heart attacks and strokes to the development of small areas of infection in the lungs. Just being on bypass causes a minimal amount of trauma to the heart and lungs, which takes some time to be restored to normal. Good nursing care and cooperation from the patient quickens the recovery time. Even with these complications, however, the risk of death from coronary bypass surgery, if performed by an experienced surgical team, *is less than 3 percent*. In higher risk patients, such as the elderly, the obese, or diabetic patients in poor condition, the mortality rate increases.

Although bypass surgery does relieve angina and ischemia, its effects don't always last forever. As long as the same lifestyle risk factors prevail, atherosclerosis can form in the bypass grafts and additional blockages can form in the coronary arteries. Some studies report up to 15 percent of all bypass grafts become obstructed within one year. However, if only one of three grafts blocks in a particular patient, a reoperation is usually not necessary. Only if new angina occurs or additional heart muscle is jeopardized does a reoperation become crucial. Generally, a routine coronary bypass operation is good for ten years. After that time, failure of the grafts may occur and a second bypass operation is often required.

Heart Transplant

Simply stated, coronary artery bypass surgery is for obstructed coronary *arteries*. Heart transplants are for destroyed heart *muscle*.

If the heart has sustained multiple heart attacks, and the muscle has been injured so severely that it can never again function properly, and there is advanced heart failure, the patient may need a heart transplant. The heart muscle may be damaged from other causes such as infection: a condition known as cardiomyopathy.

Heart transplants should no longer be considered experimental. More than 4,000 heart transplants were done worldwide in 1988, and 131 hospitals in the United States offer this service.

A successful heart transplant depends on a large team of skilled professionals. The team members include cardiac surgeons, a cardiologist, an anesthesiologist, an immunologist, an infectious diseases specialist, a social worker, a psychiatrist, and specialized nurses.

There are numerous restrictions in the selection of candidates for a heart transplant. The age limit has been eliminated in many hospitals, but some will not transplant anyone over the age of fifty. The patient must be in relatively good health, except for terminal heart failure. If a patient has diabetes, severe hypertension, kidney disease, or severely impaired lungs, he may be turned down by the transplant team.

Once approved to be a recipient, the patient is discharged from the hospital, often with a beeper, until a donor becomes available. The beeper allows doctors to contact the patient any time of day or night, no matter where the patient is, in case a heart is found. The long wait for an appropriate donor heart is the single biggest drawback of heart transplant surgery.

The biggest risks involved in heart transplantation come not during the surgery itself, but postoperatively. The body's immune system naturally attacks the foreign tissue and fights to reject the transplanted organ. But wonder drugs have now been developed to counter this problem. Cyclosporine has been the most widely used drug in recent years to stop transplant rejection before it starts. It can be used alone or in combination with other drugs such as steroids. Newer drugs are now being tested that are even more effective than cyclosporine and will probably replace it. We can thank the miracle of research and the tenacity of many physicians and scientists for bringing us to this era of safe transplant surgery. One day this knowledge will be expanded to the point where transplants from animals such as baboons may be feasible.

Along with the good these immunosuppressive agents provide, there is some bad. While cyclosporine and other such drugs prevent the immune system from attacking the new heart, they also stop the white blood cells from defending the body from its true enemies: viruses and bacteria. This can leave the patient susceptible to a wide variety of infectious diseases. Of course, there are other side effects depending on the drug used, but with judicious care they can be minimized.

The success rate of heart transplants has reached the incredible 80 percent mark at one year following surgery, making it routine where available and when needed. And more than half of all transplant patients now live for five years or more after their operation.

Healthy Prospects

Whether or not you ever develop heart disease, understanding the available treatments and recovery outlook can eliminate your fear of the unknown and provide you with a measure of confidence that heart disease is manageable. If you do find yourself or a loved one facing treatment for heart disease, you can feel confident the current techniques have been proven effective and successful time and time again. And the odds of recovering from heart disease to live a long and full life are getting better every year. Chapter 8 provides a glimpse into the future of heart disease treatment.

8

Medical Frontiers in Treatment

If you or a loved one do suffer from coronary heart disease, there is a much better chance of survival today than there was just twenty years ago. Each year brings new medical, technological, and surgical advances that improve the diagnosis and treatment of coronary artery disease. We hope you will never need to find out how far medicine and surgery have come in the last few decades. But rest assured that if you do, you will find yourself in good hands. A brief description follows of some of the present and future arsenal for the diagnosis, treatment, and prevention of heart disease.

Apo B Test

Apo B is the protein component of low-density lipoprotein (LDL) cholesterol. Preliminary studies indicate that testing for deviations in this apolipoprotein will identify people who are at a genetically high risk of developing heart disease. If individuals who have such a family history were to take this test while still young, the results might help detect the potential for heart disease giving them plenty of opportunity to adopt preventive diet and exercise programs. The apo B test is available in Europe and some areas of North America. It is expected to be widespread in the near future as a screening test.

Portable ECG Monitor

Imagine being at home, walking in your garden, or being at the shopping center and all the time having your heart rhythm monitored and computer analyzed. Such devices now exist and are being used on a limited basis for testing. When they become widely available, high-risk patients who have sustained a heart attack or arrhythmia or older folks who live alone and feel insecure about their cardiac status will be able to be constantly monitored.

The portable ECG monitor consists of a small transceiver that can be worn around the neck, similar to the type worn in the hospital for ambulatory monitoring. The ECG signal can be sent via a telephone receiver or satellite to the computer-monitoring station. If an abnormality in rhythm occurs, it is instantly recognized and appropriately communicated to your physician. If a life-threatening arrhythmia occurs, the paramedics will be notified and sent to help.

t-PA

Much of the work being done in the genetic engineering of synthetic tissue plasminogen activator (t-PA) is to make its action more specific and to avoid the generalized anticoagulation effect it has on the body. If such a chemical design of this drug can be developed, it will enable precise dissolution of already formed blood clots and avoid the potential complication of generalized bleeding.

A wonder drug this specific will be safe to administer at home or anywhere a heart attack occurs. Imagine a patient suffering a heart attack and not having to wait for medical treatment. An injection or pill of this modified t-PA might enable a clot blocking a coronary artery to be dissolved in a few minutes. Many lives would be saved by such an advance in technology. It may one day sit on the shelf of medicine cabinets next to the aspirin.

Artificial Internal Defibrillators

An occasional patient has intractable episodes of ventricular tachycardia or ventricular fibrillation. As we discussed, these arrhythmias can be lethal and the latter requires cardiopulmonary resuscitation (CPR). If the cause of these problems is coronary artery disease, bypass surgery will commonly correct the arrhythmia. If the cause is not coronary artery disease, then specific drugs or an artificial internal defibrillator (AID) will be required.

Sometimes there is an irritable focus in the heart that keeps setting off these arrhythmias, threatening the life of the patient. Other times fibrillation occurs due to extensive areas of muscle destruction in the heart, or a cardiomyopathy. These must first be treated with drugs. If repeated episodes of fibrillation occur while under drug treatment, then the patient is considered a candidate for the AID device. The AID device is a lifesaver for those who need it. Marvelous technology in recent years has reduced the standard defibrillator to an implantable device. It requires surgery to place one electrode lead on the apex of the heart and a second lead near the right atrium (see Figures 3 and 4). These two leads are connected to a small battery. Sophisticated electronics sense the rhythm of the heart, and if the rhythm turns to fibrillation, the battery sends a charge into the electrodes to defibrillate the heart. Multiple shocks are sometimes required to convert the rhythm to normal. The AID batteries must be recharged and replaced periodically depending on the number of shocks they have given.

Much work has gone into simplifying the design and implantation of the AID device. Initially surgeons had to open the chest and sew the electrodes onto the heart. Recent work has obviated the need for open chest surgery.

New configurations of the AID device are being developed that combine its function with a pacemaker, all in one unit. Sometime in the future the pacemaker will be combined with this simpler implantation system of electrodes, minimizing the amount of surgical intervention. At such time the indications for its use will expand to thousands of patients who will be able to have a standby system for defibrillation available.

Stents

In the discussion of balloon angioplasty (chapter 7) we described the problem of the arteries becoming blocked again even if the angioplasty seemed to clear them initially. The question arises as to why the artery blocks off again so quickly. Some scientists think this has to do with damage to the lining of the vessel wall causing clots to form there. Others think it has to do with the softness of the vessel wall, and still others think there is a "memory" to the vessel wall that restores it back to its blocked position. Whatever the reason, reblockage (called restenosis) is a real problem.

It is now being found that the restenosis rate can be reduced with stents. These are tiny meshlike tubular devices made of materials such as stainless steel, tantalum, and nitinol (a nickel-titanium compound). They are placed over one of the tiny balloon angioplasty catheters and inserted at the point of blockage when the angioplasty balloon is inflated. The balloon dilates the stent so that it expands to line the inner vessel wall with a hard supporting structure, thus, it is hoped, preventing restenosis.

To date the results are mixed. When a stent has been used in the larger thicker blood vessels of the leg (for example, the iliac and femoral arteries), the results have been good. When they have been used in the smaller coronary arteries, the results have not been as successful. New materials and new designs of stents are being evaluated worldwide to solve the insidious restenosis problem.

Atherectomy

The Roto-Rooter is finally here! For years people have been asking, "When are you going to clean out arteries like a plumber?" Well, we finally can. Although we use a more sophisticated term than Roto-Rooter. We call our devices atherectomy instruments.

It took the development of high-speed miniaturized motors and drills to make atherectomy devices feasible. Although this idea was being researched for years, the devices were too large, too slow, and too damaging. With miniaturization and high-speed drills, one of the basic problems was solved—how to avoid freeing pieces of plaque to float elsewhere in the blood vessel. One design, with high-speed drills rotating in excess of tens of thousands of revolutions per minute, vaporizes whatever plaque it comes in contact with. The fragments drilled off are so tiny that they are absorbed into the blood or can pass harmlessly through the vascular system. Another type cuts off and captures pieces of the plaque. These two types of atherectomy instruments are presently being clinically tested. Many other variations in design are being evaluated as well, and the technique may be brought into standard use soon.

Laser Surgery

The term laser is an acronym for light amplification by stimulated emission of radiation. Light waves are concentrated and their energy focused and controlled to perform a great range of tasks. The use of lasers to remove atherosclerotic plaque from the walls of the arteries involves the successful melding of many technologies. Many of the problems have been solved; some are still being researched.

Why lasers for vascular surgery? For two reasons. First, if a blocked blood vessel can be opened up with a laser, surgery can be avoided. Second, if it works effectively in removing plaque it might decrease the restenosis rate following balloon angioplasty. Advances in laser surgery are providing a promising breakthrough in the treatment of coronary artery disease and vascular disease elsewhere in the body.

Two basic types of lasers are being used and experimented with for vascular surgery: hot lasers and cold lasers. The hot lasers use heat, with a bare beam or simply captured in a metal cap tip, to vaporize the atherosclerotic plaque. The hot lasers are called photothermal lasers. The two most popular sources of this laser energy are the Argon and Neodynium Yag lasers.

The second type, the cold lasers, act by breaking chemical bonds in tissues. They are called photochemical lasers. The most popular one developed to date is the Excimer laser.

But do they work? Yes and no. In the larger vessels of the leg, lasers have been successful. In the coronary arteries, lasers have not worked as well. The hot laser in the heart has yielded equivocal results. The heat in these tiny vessels can open up the blockages, but the restenosis rate has not yet been decreased. The cold lasers appear more promising in solving this problem. The Excimer laser comes from an ultraviolet source and vaporizes the blockage in the artery without any heat. It also seems to work better than the hot laser on the harder plaques. Whether or not it will reduce the restenosis rate still remains to be seen, but the initial results are promising.

A combined device of balloon and laser, aptly called the Laser Balloon, is being tested in selected circumstances. This device is being evaluated in patients with abrupt closure of an artery following balloon angioplasty. Over the next year or two, this combined procedure may yield improved results over balloon catheters alone.

Laser surgery has been very public in the last few years. Each success gets media attention, and the hope for an easy and early cure-all for vascular disease is further aroused. But like all areas of research, laser surgery has taken two steps forward and one step backward. However, it *is* making progress. Surgeons, cardiologists, radiologists, engineers, and scientists are all working together to perfect laser surgical techniques. Lasers have enormous potential to defeat atherosclerosis. As they are harnessed, understood, and applied, they may eventually eliminate the need for more invasive forms of surgery.

Artificial Heart

The technological breakthrough of the 1980s, the artificial heart may someday be able to replace the human heart on a permanent basis. To achieve that goal, a totally implantable device must be perfected. Considering the multifaceted nature of the heart, the plastic substitutes have demonstrated an amazing level of technological engineering.

The first artificial heart was implanted in Dr. Barney Clark in 1982. He lived less than four months. Because this device received its power supply from outside the body, it was unwieldy and Dr. Clark was tethered to his power source.

Currently engineers and physicians are using calves to test a totally implantable artificial heart. The power supply resides in the abdomen and contains a battery that can be recharged from a power source outside the body. This design incorporates two obvious advantageous features: it leaves the patient free to go anywhere without being connected to a power source and it eliminates the need for tubes and connections that come through the skin and are a source of infection.

Until such devices are perfected, the artificial heart will be regarded only as a temporary bridge to heart transplantation. It is a life-saving stopgap, and is now widely used for that purpose. In years to come, there may be less reason for a patient to die if a donor heart is not available.

Preventing Coronary Heart Disease

Although the future holds promise for enormous improvements in diagnosing, treating, and reversing coronary artery disease, prevention is and always will be the best therapy. The steps have been clearly outlined in this book: quit smoking; adopt a low-fat, low-cholesterol, low-calorie, high-fiber diet; and incorporate regular physical activity into your life. It is better to prevent a problem than to wait until it occurs to solve it. If you haven't yet begun, start making these steps part of your life today.

Remember that in making these changes, you will not only improve your odds against the possibility of coronary and other vascular disease, but you will be a good example for your children as well. Like you, they will have increasingly better odds of living healthy and happy lives.

9

If You Want to Know More ... Resources

If you want to know more about coronary heart disease there are a great many resources to which you can turn. National and local organizations and support groups can offer a great deal of information and help. In addition, there are dozens of books, magazines, videotapes, and other media tools that can advance your knowledge of coronary heart disease. Whether it runs in your family, or you have acquired coronary or other vascular disease, or you want more in-depth information about its prevention, an enormous amount of information is available.

Organizations

Both the national and local chapters of the following associations can help provide you with information on everything from risk factors for heart disease to programs that will help you quit smoking. Look for the local chapter listed in your phone book, or contact the national headquarters:

American Heart Association
7320 Greenville Avenue
Dallas, TX 75231
(214) 373–6300

or in Canada:
Heart and Stroke Foundation of Canada
160 George Street, Suite 200
Ottawa, Ontario K1N9M2
(613) 237–4361

Your local chapter or the national headquarters of the American Heart Association or the Heart and Stroke Foundation of Canada can provide you with a great deal of information on heart disease, heart surgery, a heart-healthy diet, and exercise programs. They can also put you in contact with programs to help you quit smoking and support groups for heart disease victims and their families.

YMCA Cardiovascular Health Program
422 Ninth Avenue
New York, NY 10007
(212) 564–1300

Your local branch of the YMCA may participate in the organization's nationwide cardiovascular health program. Participating branches test both blood pressure and cholesterol levels and offer a schedule of classes in cardiopulmonary resuscitation (CPR) as well as a wide variety of aerobic exercises.

American National Red Cross
Seventeenth and D Streets
Washington, DC 20006
(202) 737–8300

Local Red Cross chapters regularly offer classes in CPR. Contact your local chapter for a schedule of classes in your area.

American Lung Association
1740 Broadway
New York, NY 10019
(212) 315–8700

The American Lung Association can provide you with literature on quitting smoking and connect you with programs that can help you quit if you can't do so on your own.

Support Groups

The Mended Hearts, Inc.
7320 Greenville Avenue
Dallas, TX 75231
(214) 706–1442

The Mended Hearts, Inc., offers much-needed support and counseling to heart surgery patients and their family members.

Many local hospitals and local organizations also sponsor programs or groups that provide support and counseling to heart patients, under a wide variety of names, from the Heart Club to the Zipper Club to Heart to Heart. Contact your local chapter of the American Heart Association, or ask your physician for more information about support groups near you.

Mass Media

Heart-Healthy Cookbooks

Cooley, Denton A., and Moore, Carolyn E. *Eat Smart for a Healthy Heart Cookbook*. New York: Barron's, 1987.

DeBakey, Michael. *The Living Heart Diet*. New York: Simon & Schuster, 1984.

Esheleman, Ruth, and Winston, Mary, compilers. *The American Heart Association Cookbook*. New York: Ballantine Books, 1984.

Goor, Ronald S., and Goor, Nancy. *Eater's Choice: A Food Lover's Guide to Lower Cholesterol*. Boston, MA: Houghton Mifflin, 1989.

Other Helpful Books for Prevention and Treatment of Heart Disease

American Heart Association. *Heartbook: A Guide to Prevention and Treatment of Cardiovascular Diseases*. New York: E. P. Dutton, 1980.

American National Red Cross. *Cardiopulmonary Resuscitation*. Washington, DC: American National Red Cross, 1974.

Cooper, Kenneth. *Overcoming Hypertension*. New York: Bantam, 1990.

Gaskin, John. *The Heart*. New York: Franklin Watts, 1985.

Gasner, Douglas, and McCleary, Elliott H. *The American Medical Association Guide to HeartCare*. New York: Random House, 1984.

Horovitz, Emmanuel. *Heartbeat: A Complete Guide to Understanding and Preventing Heart Disease*. Encino, CA: Health Trend Publishing, 1988.

Khan, M. Gabriel. *Heart Attacks, Hypertension, and Heart Drugs*. Emmaus, PA: Rodale Press, 1987.

Klieman, Charles. *Save Your Arteries, Save Your Life*. New York: Warner Books, 1987.

Ornish, Dean.* *Program for Reversing Heart Disease*. New York: Random House, 1990.

Silverstein, Alvin, and Silverstein, Virginia B. *Heartbeats: Your Body, Your Heart*. Philadelphia: J. B. Lippincott Co., 1983.

Silverstein, Alvin, and Silverstein, Virginia B. *Heart Disease: America's #1 Killer*. Philadelphia: J. B. Lippincott Co., 1985.

Tiger, Stephen. *Heart Disease*. New York: Julian Messner, 1986.

Williams, Redford. *The Trusting Heart: Great News about Type A Behavior*. New York: Times Books, 1989.

Yalof, Ina L. *Open Heart Surgery: A Guidebook for Patients and Families*. New York: Random House, 1983.

---

*Dr. Dean Ornish's research shows that even severe coronary heart disease can often be reversed by making comprehensive changes in diet and lifestyle. His study showed that patients who made such changes (a 10 percent fat vegetarian diet, stress management techniques, and moderate exercise), after only one year, had a 91 percent decrease in the frequency of chest pain, whereas pain increased in the comparison group. More important, the coronary artery blockages reversed in 82 percent of the patients (from 61.1 percent to 55.8 percent) in the group that followed Dr. Ornish's program, whereas the blockages increased (from 61.7 percent to 64.4 percent) in the majority of patients who made more moderate changes.

Pamphlets and Booklets

Superintendent of Documents
U.S. Government Printing Office
Washington, DC 20402

The U.S. Government Printing Office (USGPO) will provide you a catalog of all of their book titles and information on pamphlets published by the National Heart, Lung and Blood Institute if you send a written request. Most of the pamphlets cost between 25 cents and a couple of dollars. Four very helpful USGPO pamphlets are:

Eating to Lower Your High Blood Cholesterol
Exercise and Your Heart
Heart Healthy Handbook for Women
So You Have High Blood Cholesterol

The American Heart Association (address on p. 138) also publishes a number of helpful booklets. Ask for the following titles:

The American Heart Association Diet
CPR in Basic Life Support
How to Make Your Heart Last a Lifetime

Periodicals

The Diet-Heart Newsletter
820 Crestmoore Place
Venice, CA 90291

Heart to Heart
Associates in Medical Marketing Co.
9 Pheasant Run Road
Newtown, PA 18940

Video and Television Shows

Cardiology Update. This weekly program, directed primarily toward physicians and other professionals, provides a great deal of information that nonprofessionals might find fascinating. It airs Sundays on the LIFETIME cable network. Check your local listings for times.

My Heart, Your Heart. MacNeil-Lehrer-Gannett Productions. (Washington, DC: PBS Video)

Just for Children

Filmstrips
For the Sake of Your Heart. Pleasantville, NY: Sunburst Communications, 1980.
The Physiology of Exercise. Pleasantville, NY: Sunburst Communications, 1976.

Glossary

Angina Pectoris. Also called *angina*. A pressure or chest-crushing pain caused by a deprivation of oxygen to the heart.

Angiogram. See *Coronary Angiogram*.

Angioplasty. Also called *percutaneous transluminal coronary angioplasty* (PTCA). A procedure to widen the coronary artery at its point of blockage. The inflation of a small balloon inside an artery compresses atherosclerotic plaque against arterial walls, resulting in greater blood flow to the heart.

Apolipoprotein B-100. Also called *apo B*. The protein component of low-density lipoproteins, which carry cholesterol through the bloodstream to various parts of the body. A possible indicator of coronary disease.

Arrhythmia. Any deviation from the normal rhythm of the heart.

Atherosclerosis. The buildup of deposits on the inner wall of arteries composed primarily of cholesterol and fat (lipids). There may or may not be calcium deposits in atherosclerotic plaque.

Atrium. One of two chambers of the heart that collect blood. The right atrium collects oxygen-depleted blood from the body, then passes it into the right ventricle, which pumps it to the lungs. The left atrium collects oxygen-rich blood from the lungs, then passes it into the left ventricle, which pumps it through the body's circulatory system.

Bradycardia. An arrhythmia in which the heart beats slowly.

Cardiac Arrhythmia. See *Arrhythmia*.

Cardiac Catheterization. A surgical procedure in which a catheter is snaked through the body's blood vessels to the heart. Used to provide images of the heart at work.

Cardiopulmonary Resuscitation (CPR). A definitive technique for restarting the heart and restoring breathing in someone who has suffered a cardiac or respiratory arrest. Important for everyone to know.

Cholesterol. A yellowish, waxy lipid used by the body in the production of hormones, nerve fibers, and cell membranes. It is found in animal cells and is produced in the liver. It is the primary component of atherosclerotic buildup that can lead to heart disease.

Congestive Heart Failure. See *Heart Failure*.

Coronary Angiogram. The X-ray procedure done during *cardiac catheterization*. Dye is injected into the coronary arteries and recorded on film or videotape.

Coronary Arteries. The blood vessels that supply the heart muscle with oxygen and nourishment.

Diabetes Mellitus. A chronic elevation of blood sugar levels due to an inability to process glucose efficiently.

Diastolic. The second number in a blood pressure reading. The period in the cardiac cycle when the ventricles fill with blood. Reflects the degree of resistance in the peripheral arteries.

Echocardiogram. A diagnostic test that uses the reflection of ultrasonic sound waves to provide images of the heart. This test can be done at rest or during exercise.

Electrocardiogram. A diagnostic test that reflects the electrical activity of the heart. Used to diagnose normal or abnormal rhythms, decreased oxygen to the heart (ischemia), heart attacks, and numerous other heart conditions.

Exercise Stress Test. A diagnostic test used to measure the heart's ability to withstand stress and the coronary arteries' capacity to provide the heart muscle with the supply of blood it needs. Usually performed on a treadmill.

Fibrillation, Ventricular. Irregular contractions of the heart muscle in which the heart rhythm is ineffective in pumping blood. Fatal if not converted to a regular rhythm within a few minutes.

Fractionation. See *Lipoprotein-Cholesterol Fractionation*.

Heart Attack. Also called a *myocardial infarction*. Due to blockage of one of the coronary arteries with resultant necrosis (death) of the muscle tissue supplied by that blocked artery. The leading cause of death in the United States and Canada.

Heart Failure. Also called *congestive heart failure*. Due to enough damage done to the heart muscle that it can't function properly for the demands of the body. The heart muscle does not pump satisfactorily, leading to a buildup of fluid in the lungs and body tissues. Manifested by shortness of breath and edema in the legs and abdomen.

High-Density Lipoproteins (HDL). The "good" kind of cholesterol. Transports cholesterol to the liver for disposal. Composed of high concentration of protein and low concentration of cholesterol. High levels of HDL are associated with a lower incidence of atherosclerosis.

Holter Monitor. A portable device that measures the electrocardiogram over 24 or 48 hours.

Hypercholesterolemia. A cholesterol level over 260 mg/dl. A high-risk factor for atherosclerosis.

Hypertension. A blood pressure reading over 160/95. Borderline hypertension is between 140/90 and 160/95. A high-risk factor for atherosclerosis.

Ischemia. An inadequate supply of oxygen to any area of the body.

Lasers. An acronym standing for light amplification by stimulated emission of radiation. A high-energy source of light used to clear clogged arteries.

Lipoprotein. A molecule of fat and protein that transports cholesterol through the bloodstream.

Lipoprotein-Cholesterol Fractionation. A test used to determine the levels of LDL and HDL fractions of cholesterol in the blood.

Low-Density Lipoproteins (LDL). The "bad" kind of cholesterol that contains low concentrations of protein and high concentrations of cholesterol. High levels are associated with atherosclerosis.

Monounsaturated Fats. These oils come from plants, contain few hydrogen atoms, and are liquid at room temperature.

Myocardial Infarction. See *Heart Attack*.

Plaque. Hardened deposits of fat and cholesterol on the inside lining of blood vessels. The buildup of plaques of atherosclerosis cause coronary artery disease.

Plasminogen Activator. A substance in plasma that activates the dissolution of blood clots.

Polyunsaturated Fats. These fats come from plants, contain fewer hydrogen atoms than monounsaturates, and are liquid at room temperature.

Saturated Fats. These fats come from animals, contain a high number of hydrogen atoms, and are solid at room temperature.

Silent Ischemia. Ischemia without symptoms. Lack of oxygen to the heart from coronary artery disease that produces no outward signs of the disease.

Streptokinase. An enzyme derived from *Streptococcus* used to dissolve acutely occurring blood clots.

Systolic. The first number in a blood pressure reading. Measures the force of contraction of the heart.

Tachycardia. An arrhythmia in which the heart beats rapidly.

Thallium Imaging. A diagnostic test to measure the amount of oxygen supply to the heart muscle. A small amount of a radioactive material is injected into the bloodstream and followed by a special scanner to determine the amount of uptake in the heart.

t-PA. Tissue plasminogen activator. Genetically engineered drug to dissolve blood clots.

Urokinase. An enzyme derived from urine to dissolve acutely occurring blood clots.

About the Authors

Dr. Charles Klieman is a cardiovascular and thoracic surgeon. He is board certified in surgery, thoracic and cardiovascular surgery, and laser surgery and has received qualification for special board certification in vascular surgery. He is founder and director of the Laser Center at Presbyterian Intercommunity Hospital, Whittier, California, and director of the Vascular Center at Whittier Hospital. He is author of the book *Save Your Arteries, Save Your Life* (Warner Books, 1987). An inventor of numerous patented vascular surgical devices, he is currently in private practice in Los Angeles.

Kevin Osborn, a free-lance writer and editor, has authored or coauthored more than a dozen books for adults and children. Many of his adult titles—most recently *Lonely All the Time,* which he wrote with doctors Ralph Earle and Gregory Crowe—focus on issues of health and psychological well-being, particularly regarding alcoholism and other addictions.

C. Scott McMillin is the director of the Suburban Hospital Addiction Treatment Center and an adjunct faculty member at the University of Virginia. He is the co-author of numerous books, including *Don't Help: A Positive Guide to Working with the Alcoholic* and *The Twelve Steps Revisited.*

Index

Angiotensin (hormone), 89
  converting enzyme (ACE) inhibitors,
    87, 89
Apo A, 12
Apo B, 12, 128
  defined, 145
  test, 128
Apolipoprotein B-100. *See* Apo B
Apoprotein, 12
Apostat, 61
Argon laser. *See* Lasers, hot
Arryhthmia, 47, 86, 98–99, 101, 105,
    106, 112, 128, 130
  bradycardia, 98–99, 116, 146
  correcting, 116–117, 129–130
  defined, 145
  fibrillation, 99
  and heart attacks, 86, 98–99
  tachycardia, 98
  ventricular fibrillation, 99, 112, 129
  ventricular tachycardia, 99, 129
Artery. *See also* Angioplasty; Heart at-
    tack
  blockage. *See* Clots; Heart attack
  brachial, 109
  carotid, 12
  coronary, 146
    disease, xi, 33, 84–85, 127, 129,
      133
  femoral, 109, 131
  iliac, 131
  illustrations, 94, 95
Artificial heart, 134–135
Artificial internal defibrillator (AID),
    129–130
Aspirin, 89–91, 119–120, 129
  British study, 89–90
  U.S. physicians study, 89
Asymptomatic people, 105
Atherectomy, 132
Atherosclerosis, xi, xii, xiv, 3, 9, 11, 12–
    13, 16–18, 20, 22, 26, 30, 31, 39,
    47, 96–98
  angioplasty, 90, 112, 116, 118, 131
  blockage, 7, 18, 131
  blood disorders and, 83–84
  bypass surgery and, 116, 118, 120–
    122
  cholesterol and, 31–32
  controlling, 9, 71–73
  coronary heart disease and, 3–4
  crash diets and, 62
  defined, 146
  diagnosing, 105
  dietary fats and, 5, 62, 64, 86, 87, 135
  genetic causes, 11, 12–13, 16–19
  HDL and, 84–85

smoking and, xi–xii, 2, 5, 6–7, 11, 15,
    22, 24, 27, 28–29, 33, 35, 39, 48,
    49, 51, 52–54, 55, 65, 74, 80, 83,
    85, 86, 87, 91, 96, 97, 114
Atrium, 94,146

Bacteria (and surgery), 124
"Bad" cholesterol. *See* Low-density lipo-
    proteins (LDL)
Baked goods, commercial, 57, 64
Balloon angioplasty. *See* Angioplasty
Basketball, 41
Beef. *See* Meat
Beta-blockers, 32, 88, 113, 116
Bicycling, xiii, 41
Bile acids, 7, 67, 85
Birth control pills. *See* Oral contracep-
    tives
Bleeding
  brain, 115
  gastrointestinal tract, 115
  internal, 90
Blockage, artery. *See* Heart attack
Blood
  abnormal clotting, 7
  clots, xii, 9, 18, 29, 48, 69, 90, 114,
    115, 119–120, 129
    busters, 114–116, 129
  disorders and atherosclerosis, 83–84
  lipid abnormality, 83–84
  plasminogen activator, low, 18, 114,
    115, 129, 149
  platelets, 29, 69, 90
  pressure, 30, 31, 51, 74
    and adrenaline, 43
    and angiotension, 89
    diastolic, 30, 31, 74
    and meditation, 80
    monitor, 30
    systolic, 30, 31, 74
  sugars, 17
    exercise and, 63
    high, 27, 39
    testing, 39
  transfusions, 121
  vessel
    injury, 118
    and prostacyclin, 48
Books for prevention and treatment of
    heart disease, 140–141
Borderline hypertension, 30
Brachial artery, 109
Bradycardia, 98–99, 116, 146. *See also*
    Arrhythmia
Brain
  apostat, 61
  bleeding, 115